THE PUBLIC POETRY OF ROBERT LOWELL

THE PUBLIC POETRY
OF
ROBERT LOWELL

by

Patrick Cosgrave

LONDON
VICTOR GOLLANCZ LTD
1970

© Patrick Cosgrave 1970

ISBN 0 575 00539 4

PRINTED IN GREAT BRITAIN
BY EBENEZER BAYLIS AND SON LTD
THE TRINITY PRESS, WORCESTER, AND LONDON

To
My Mother
and
The Memory of my Father

Contents

Preface

A WORD ABOUT the scope and purpose of this book may not be out of order.

Both as regards weakness and strength I have felt for a long time that the poetry of our own day has not received the kind of scrutiny it deserves and that we need, that is, scrutiny in the light of both poetic theory and of the tradition. I have tried, therefore, to write a study of a single modern poet where the words on the page will be examined, not only for themselves but in relation to a consistent theory of poetics and of literary history. I have tried (as I hope Chapter Six will make clear) not to allow my appreciation of the tradition to blind me to the merits of modern verse; but I have tried as well not to be beguiled by poetry of my own time, the ideology as well as the style of which (as I suggest in Chapters One and Four) seems to have had a corrupting effect on many modern critics. Briefly, I hope this book will provide a series of readings of and judgements about our most remarkable living poet that are well-grounded in that they relate as thoroughly as I can make them to what seems to me to be the only tenable theory of poetics as well as to a sound view of the history of the tradition. In so far as the reader disagrees with either theory or history he will probably disagree with my judgements. But I am certain that I have, in principle, chosen the right way to go about the business; to relate, that is, the subject of the study to a definition of poetry and an account of the history.

I have, however, tried to integrate theory, history and meaning as we go along. I have not, that is, set out a theory and a history and then applied them to texts. Rather, after Chapter One particularly, I have tried to dovetail general discussion with the chronology of Lowell's career. In this way the reader will come across the general as well as the local argument roughly in the order in which I myself came across them in the nine years in which I have been studying the subject and the two and a half during which this book was being written. At each stage at which a judgement raises a difficulty, historical and theoretical discussion are to be found in its proximity.

The historical theory in Chapter One is, I believe, largely original. The moral and absolutist theory of poetry expounded in the book is not. It is, I believe, the theory on which English literature is founded, but it will be immediately apparent to the reader that I have been most influenced in my account of it by the work of the man whom I regard as incomparably the greatest critic of this century, the late Yvor Winters.

On the other hand, I do not always agree with Winters. The place which Yeats occupies in these pages, the actual expression of my own theories of poetry, particularly in Chapters Three and Six, and the animadversions on Winters in Chapter Six, will demonstrate that. The first and third of these disagreements are not fully worked out in the following pages because, however desirable I felt a general account of my reasoning to be, I could not feel justified in overloading my pages with it to the exclusion of Lowell. I hope, therefore, that I have not at any stage lost my focus.

I would like to say a further word about what has been left out. In Chapter One the reader will find an historical division of English poetry into the line of gravity and the line of wit. The former is made to depend on Samuel Johnson. I have not given a full account of my reading of Johnson, though I hope to do so in the future. In Chapter One and Chapter Six particularly the reader will find the following argument. In modern poetry Eliot and Pound belong to the line of wit, Yeats and Lowell to the line of gravity. In his most recent work, and particularly in 'Waking Early Sunday Morning', in my view his greatest and one of the greatest as well as the most important for the future of contemporary poems, Lowell has gone clearly over, technically as well as spiritually, to the inheritance of Yeats. In doing so he has finally abandoned the corrupting influence on him of the school of Eliot, a school which has come near to ruining modern poetry in English but which, with 'Waking Early Sunday Morning', may well be on the point of final exclusion from influence in the development of English literature: I hope profoundly that this is so. The reader may see, in my denunciation of Eliot, the most marked sign of the influence of Winters; he will not see any comparable influence in the elevation of Yeats, whom I regard as incomparably the greatest and most important of modern poets, the establishment of whose absolute centrality cannot be much longer delayed. Not all of this argument is by any means fully explored in the book and must be reserved for future writing. I believe, however, that I have given sufficient reasons for the reader to judge of my argument. For example, I believe that any moderately sensitive reader who agrees with my account of the greatness of 'Waking Early Sunday Morning' has only to take down a volume of Yeats's later poetry and read it instantly to grasp the general nature of my argument. Nonetheless, my general ideas have been explored only in so far as they are consistent with maintaining the focus on Lowell. I hope this study may be a foundation brick for later work that will explain more fully all the elements in my thinking and thus help in the establishment of a general theory and account of modern poetry the various elements in which will support each other to the satisfaction of the reader concerned to convince himself of the consistency of my views even if he cannot agree with them.

Like any student of Lowell I owe much to the pioneers who have written on him. In particular I owe a great debt to Mr. Hugh B. Staples, even though I disagree with him more often than not. The greatest debt I owe, however, is to Professor Denis Donoghue. It was he who, some years ago, introduced me to the work of Winters, and such merit as I have as a critic of poetry I owe to the rigorous discipline of continual argument over texts in University College, Dublin, when I was a pupil of his. He has not read this book, and may be surprised at its emergence. Nonetheless, and whether he agrees with it or not, he is its first inspiration: his kindness, pertinacity, omnivorous knowledge and courtesy in disputation I will never forget, as I will ever recall his inspired teaching.

Other friends have contributed in many ways. I put them down in no sort of order. Miss Eavan Boland, whose brilliant poetry demonstrates the continued vigour of the tradition of Yeats in Ireland, has inspired me alike to violent assent and violent dissent on many occasions. Over the years, both Mr. Liam Hourican and Dr. Dermot Fenlon, both products, in their way, of the very best teaching of University College, Dublin, have guided and refined my arguments and crushed in a salutary fashion an often thoughtless ebullience of argument. During the writing of this book, and particularly at its most difficult stages, my niece, Neasa, gave me unstinted and vigorous support and encouragement. All these debts I owe in multiple measure to my wife, Ruth, as I owe her much else besides. I am particularly grateful to Mrs. Diane Pledger, who on this as on many other projects, has grappled nobly and successfully, not only with my handwriting, but with the vagaries of my working temperament; to Mr. James McGuire for his brilliance as a Quarter Master General, and to Dr. Ronan Fanning, who devoted much valuable time to reading and commenting on the whole manuscript with acumen and perspicacity. Mr. Giles Gordon of Gollancz has waited too long for this book but has been the acme of patience and consideration throughout, while my agent, Mr. Hilary Rubinstein, by bringing order into my affairs, finally made the project possible.

Finally, I should like to express my thanks to Messrs. Faber & Faber, Lowell's publishers in this country, for permission to quote extensively from his work.

The Poems of Robert Lowell

1944: *Land of Unlikeness* (Massachusetts).
1946: *Lord Weary's Castle* (New York).
1950: *Poems 1938–49* (London, 2nd ed. 1960).
1951: *The Mills of the Kavanaughs* (New York, 1951).
1959: *Life Studies* (London, 2nd ed. 1968).
1962: *Imitations* (London).
1965: *For the Union Dead* (London).
1967: *Near the Ocean* (London).

Poems 1938–49 contains the complete contents of *Lord Weary's Castle*; it also contains the complete contents of *The Mills of the Kavanaughs* with the exception of the title poem. This poem—'The Mills of the Kavanaughs'—is printed in full as an appendix to Hugh B. Staples' critical study, *Robert Lowell: The First Twenty Years*.

I   An Unblemished Adam

OF LOWELL R. P. Blackmur once wrote:

> '... in dealing with men his faith compels him to be fractiously vindictive, and in dealing with faith, his experience of men compels him to be nearly blasphemous.'[1]*

Blackmur was, of course, speaking essentially of the earlier poetry of Lowell, mainly of the work now contained in *Poems 1938–49*. There are also *Imitations*, *For the Union Dead* and *Life Studies* to be considered, as well as the more recent volume, *Near the Ocean*. Each of these is at least a modulation of the earlier work and *Life Studies* was seen to be (and was welcomed as) a totally new departure in the poet's work: its frequently quiet (though often despairing) and even tone of reminiscence contrasted starkly with the apocalyptic violence of *Poems 1938–49*. Still, though the areas of concern had shifted, the concerns themselves were the same in *Life Studies* as before.

True, a new dimension had been added by the psycho-therapeutic emphasis on the poet's personality, while the history of his (publicly at least) distinguished family was, in *Life Studies*, woven into his work in the same way as apocalyptic religious visions had been hitherto. And, when *Near the Ocean* appeared in 1967, we were confirmed in the view that Lowell had not essentially changed. He seemed a little drained of energy, the note of the verse as it struck the ear was less turbulent, subject to a calmer discipline, not wound up in a tight spring to the point of explosion like these lines (from 'Colloquy in Black Rock'):

> Here the jack-hammer jabs into the ocean;
> My heart, you race and stagger and demand

* Notes on page 213.

> More blood-gangs for your nigger-brass percussions,
> Till I, the stunned machine of your devotion,
> Clanging upon this cymbal of a hand,
> Am rattled screw and footloose.

The violence of Lowell's attack on his experience is much in evidence in these lines. Consider also, by way of elucidating the vision that violence is intended to convey, these lines from 'The First Sunday in Lent' (an important and characteristic poem to which I will return):

> Lord, from the lust and dust thy will destroys
> Raise an unblemished Adam who will see
> The limbs of the tormented chestnut tree
> Tingle, and hear the March-winds lift and cry:
> 'The Lord of Hosts will overshadow us.'

In *Near the Ocean* there was less incantation, less ritual and less overt violence, but the same vision of ruined man dominated. A characteristic and much-quoted passage came to be regarded as an encapsulation of Lowell's life theme:

> Pity the planet, all joy gone
> from this sweet volcanic cone;
> peace to our children when they fall
> in small war on the heels of small
> war—until the end of time
> to police the earth, a ghost
> orbiting forever lost
> in our monotonous sublime.

I am concerned here only with the general characteristics of Lowell's work and in dealing with them one can now see that Blackmur's early insight was crucial. He detected not only the violence—the personal violence—inherent in Lowell's attack on experience, but also the extreme measures to which it led the poet. The apocalyptic vision either compels or revolts; it either carries one off in a mad whirligig of emotion and incantation or it throws one back from so insistently destructive a vision of life. But the 'unblemished Adam' is never identified or described and the heart of his religion (in 'The Quaker Graveyard at Nantucket') is deliberately displeasing and unencouraging, not only in the words used to describe the Virgin Mary, but in the flat, dead run of the lines: we are asked to assent to the message of a religious vision the poet claims to see but disdains to describe:

> Our Lady, too small for her canopy,
> Sits near the altar. There's no comeliness
> At all or charm in that expressionless
> Face with its heavy eye lids. As before,
> This face, for centuries a memory,
> *Non est species, neque decor,*
> Expressionless, expresses God:

Of course such a survey of general characteristics is unfair: both 'Mother Marie Therese' and 'Skunk Hour' testify effectively to positive surges of life, the one aristocratic, the other primitive, as do other poems.

But the assertion of life is often tangential, while the main energy is employed for purposes of annunciation—annunciation which was originally religious. Lowell's admiration for human character is wry and a little unwilling: it is wrung from him

> Christ enticed
> Her heart that fluttered, while she whipped her hounds
> Into the quicksands of her manor grounds
> . . .
> She half-renounced by Candle, Book and Bell
> Her flowers and fowling pieces for the Church.
> —*Mother Marie Therese*

There is a distinct sympathy here between poet and character, as there is in many of Lowell's family poems. (I have chosen 'Mother Marie Therese' for purposes of illustration, not only because of the detail and complexity of its organisation and for Lowell's capacity to shift delicately through different moods that is shown there, but because the family poems—like 'In Memory of Arthur Winslow' in the same volume—present a different series of problems, while the familial relationships from which they arise obscure an attempt to define general characteristics.)

In *Poems 1938-49* in particular, however, Lowell demonstrates, in dealing with individual human experience, a distinct hauteur, a distancing of himself from the sordidities of life, which may be his most distinct legacy from his Bostonian cultural inheritance. Indeed, his disdain, which often turns to disgust, is never more evident than when, in dealing with his ancestors he discovers— often with amazement—the gap between their pretensions, the religious and cultural pretensions of New England, and their actual achievement:

> I came to mourn you, not to praise the craft
> That netted you a million dollars,
> . . .
> for what else could bring
> You, Arthur, to the veined and alien West
> But devil's notions that your gold at least
> Could give back life to men who whipped or backed the King?
> —*In memory of Arthur Winslow*

Lowell shows affection for individuals in his family history but he is obliged always, even when he is not raging at the hypocrisy and determined brutality that gave New England birth (as in 'Concord') to 'place' them—and thus diminish them—because they do not meet the terrible standards set for the 'unblemished Adam'. This critical alienation from his heritage has had profound effects on Lowell, for it has meant that the New England and family material which forms so great a part of his work, is never or rarely central to the ambition and drive that characterises his best as well as his weakest poetry. It is not so much, indeed, that his disdain and disgust come between him and quotidian experience (no modern poet uses the *bric-à-brac* of life more richly or rewardingly) but that they come between him and a just judgement of experience: common sense alone would revolt against so total a claim that the historical and individual activities of men were so

profoundly against the grain of the search for God which New
England believed characterised its history and which Lowell has
said dominates all poetry. But Lowell could not, in his earlier
work, achieve a morally balanced understanding of the strengths
and frailties of men because of the religious demons that whipped
him on in the search for the loudest possible religious affirmation:

> How sharp
> The burden of the Law before the beast:
> Time and the grindstone and the knife of God.
> The Child is born in blood, O child of blood
> —*New Year's Day*

And yet that task was impossible: this Lowell sometimes felt

> Is there no way to cast my hook
> Out of this dynamited brook?
> —*The Drunken Fisherman*

More, any appreciation of his often civilised ambiguity—an
ambiguity which, I have suggested, is partly a failure to come to
judgement, partly a result of the barrier Lowell's temperament
places between himself and the possibility of judging experience—
ought to encompass the horror, the full savage blackness of life
that Lowell sometimes sees:

> You damned
> My arm that cast your house upon your head
> And broke the chimney flintlock on your skull.
> . . .
> When the clubbed flintlock broke my father's brain.
> —*Rebellion*

And

> My hopped up husband drops his home disputes,
> and hits the streets to cruise for prostitutes,
> free-lancing out along the razor's edge.

> This screwball might kill his wife, then take the pledge.
> —'*To speak of the woe that is in marriage*'

And

> My mind's not right.
>
> A car radio bleats,
> 'Love, O careless Love . . .' I hear
> my ill-spirit sob in each blood cell,
> as if my hand were at its throat . . .
> I myself am hell,
> nobody's here—
> —*Skunk Hour*

True, 'Skunk Hour' ends with a fierce affirmation of life:

> a mother skunk with her column of kittens swills the garbage pail.
> She jabs her wedge head in a cup
> of sour cream, drops her ostrich tail,
> and will not scare.

But one feels that, fierce though it is, this affirmation is not positive, is, after all, something less than affirmation: coming as it does at the end, with crowding behind, an accumulation of, not mere horrors, but horrors thrown in the reader's face by a poet baring the last and deepest privations of his personality, it is a gesture of despair as much as an act of hope. The very exactness of physical description in the last stanza, the precise notation of detail—*sour* cream, *ostrich* tail—shows a poet still fully in command of the faculty of describing his own disintegration. The exactness and discipline with which that observing faculty works, almost, he persuades us for a moment, as a reflex action, is what both drives home the lunatic horror of the poet's predicament and makes us see that the final affirmation is no more than an acknowledgement by the man that the poet is still writing: but the word 'skunk' itself gives the clue to an inner feeling on his part that the act of writing holds no hope. The line 'and will not scare' becomes a diminuendo as much as it is something shot out from between clenched teeth. It is, at best, whistling in the dark.

It was work like this that led Rosenthal, in his useful commentary,[2] to express the feeling that some poetic worlds were too private for even the critic to enter into. In 'Skunk Hour' Lowell has gone on from saying (what was the message of *Poems 1938–49*) that man is ruined, to saying, with all but an ounce of his energy, that he is ruined himself.

For all the richness and variety of his work, its tapestries of learning and humour, its echoing allusions and complex analogies (all of which I will discuss in later chapters), one feels beyond a reservation that the apocalypse of 'Colloquy in Black Rock' and the terror of 'Skunk Hour' are Lowell at fullest stretch. Thus Blackmur's original insight into the violence of his temperament and the overreaching of effort it had led him to is confirmed by the later work.

It seems to me a great pity that the centrality of this judgement was not noted by the author of another most important commentary on Lowell, John Holloway.[3] Although it has often been said that Lowell, like many contemporaries immeasurably inferior to him, is a public poet, in that he deals with public themes, like Vietnam and the Presidency of the United States, no one before Holloway managed to emphasise sufficiently the importance and full meaning of that statement. Holloway began by quoting Lowell's preface to *Near the Ocean*, a collection of new pieces, along with some imitations of the classics and other poets, including a rendering of Juvenal's Tenth Satire. Lowell said

'The theme that connects my translations is Rome, the greatness and horror of her Empire . . . How one jumps from Rome to the America of my own poems is something of a mystery to me.'

Holloway denied that there was any mystery. With numerous examples, and particularly by tracing and connecting the allusions in 'Falling Asleep over the Aeneid'—in which an old man's dream enables Lowell to bring together in a moving poetic analogy events from the times of Aeneas, Carthage, Augustus and

Virgil and the American war of independence—he says that
Lowell

'. . . raises the whole position of the poet as not simply moralist, but
moral historian: as bringing his sense of values to bear not simply on
the immediate sensuous pabulum of direct experience, but on that as
it has grown from its remote past—history. The moment that a
poet, or anyone else, attempts to exercise the moral sensibility in this
way, he employs a new fundamental idea, one we have almost
ceased to think of in the context of poetry. The immediacy of our
experience is personal. What is personal may also be expressed so
that the result is universal. "This man" becomes Everyman. But the
emergence, over history, of men's present from their past is neither
of these. History is not the realm of the personal, nor the universal:
it is the realm of the public.'

But, although Holloway must be credited with the particular
central emphasis he gave to the public character of Lowell's
poetry, most of the definition quoted above, which he used to
support that emphasis, is nonsense. It is true that we have almost
ceased to think of public affairs in the context of poetry; it is also
true, but imprecise in the extreme, that earlier, public, poets
(Pope, Johnson and many Augustans as well as, in our own time,
Yeats) did bring a sense of values to bear on history; but the
imprecision of language and the obscurity of argument with
which, in the rest of this quotation, Holloway tries to relate these
activities to Lowell's work reveals that he has thought out neither
the implications of his own argument nor the true description one
ought to offer of Lowell as a 'public' poet.

By inference, Holloway recognised the inadequacy of his case
in the analysis he offered of 'Falling Asleep over the Aeneid'. The
trouble was that, although he recognised the central importance
of Lowell's 'public' ambition, and although he was aware (when
he said that this was something 'we have almost ceased to think of
in the context of poetry') that public poetry had been achieved in
the past, he had no models, no predecessors, no tradition in mind
(despite numerous classical references, and one or two to Pope
and Swift) against which he could judge and through which he

could examine the quality of Lowell's achievement. Looking at Lowell *in vacuo*, Holloway saw what the poet was trying to do, but was insufficiently critical about how well he did it.

To do him due credit, Holloway did say of 'Falling Asleep over the Aeneid', that 'there is yet a great flaw' in the poem, to be found in its use of historical analogy. This is precisely the point. The experience of the old man is placed in analogy by Lowell with Aeneas, Turnus, Augustus, the Thirteen States, Virgil, Carthage and the poet himself: one can, as Holloway says, 'see only that there is *some* analogy' not what it is:

> At the end of time,
> He sets his spear, as my descendants climb
> The knees of Father Time, his beard of scalps,
> His scythe, the arc of steel that crowns the Alps.
> The elephants of Carthage hold those snows,
> Turms of Numidian horse unsling their bows,
> The flaming turkey-feathered arrows swarm
> Beyond the Alps.

One wants, of course, to do justice to the delicate tracery of ambiguity and suggestiveness, with which Lowell embroiders his fantasy and to the sturdy power of his metrical structure. But the fact remains that in this poem the public ambition of Lowell fails, because it is quite unclear what he is saying, as it fails in some other poems discussed earlier, because of the simplistic ferocity of his vision. I do not want to suggest for a moment that any of these poems are total failures—they seem to me to be far in advance of nearly all contemporary work—but that in his central ambition as a public poet Lowell has rarely succeeded, for reasons that can be defined with relative simplicity and clarity. This definition I hope to achieve—as I hope to describe his unquestionable and considerable merits—as the argument proceeds.

I hope that, by now, I have established two general points, with which, indeed, the attentive reader of Lowell should be familiar already. Firstly, an inherent violence—moral in appearance, probably partly psychological in origin—is inseparable from Lowell's work at its fullest stretch. Secondly, though this violence

is highly personal—even his religious views were nearly heretical
—the true ambition of the poet is public; that is, he burns to judge
men and affairs against an immutable and objective standard. The
work is public, too, in a more obvious sense, in that much of it
deals with the world of politics and public affairs.

It seems to me that both of these points are obvious and, once
their centrality is established, not very interesting. The interest
lies, first in pursuing their ramifications in the poetry itself, and
then in judging the effectiveness with which Lowell has used his
two impulses. In order to carry out these two tasks it is necessary
to scrutinise the poetry minutely. But it is also necessary to set it
in the context of the past, to place it in the great tradition of public
poetry. To do this requires that we indulge in a certain amount of
intellectual history. To do that—to explain the complexity of a
poet's background—is always an extremely difficult task to carry
out at the same time as one is trying to judge his work—trying to
say, abstractly, how good it is.

One of the major difficulties of literature in the present day is
that we are now suffering almost the full effects of a serious break
in critical continuity. This is a break which began to become
apparent only recently—I would say just after the publication of
Johnson's *Lives of the Poets*. It began to be noticeable in the professional hostility of the Romantic to the Augustan tradition. Its
presence is very noticeable in the life work of Yvor Winters
whose judgement was that, with Romanticism (though he
thought much of the eighteenth century decadent and preferred
the sixteenth and seventeenth centuries) the decline of English
literature became headlong. Its presence, too, is very noticeable
in the quality of the work of F. R. Leavis: although Leavis (in my
opinion second only to Winters in quality of judgement of
individual works, though both err most catastrophically on the
work of Yeats, perhaps the only really great poet since the eighteenth century) did some of his best work on the pre-Romantics,
and was associated with the fine work of Dr. Q. D. Leavis on
Jane Austen, his heart and the main drive of his criticism has gone
into the modern novel, and there is then a lack on his part of a
total view of the literature he has studied.

Eliot was essentially an inspirational critic: though he read verse well, he never tackled it with the stubborn and ferocious moral intensity of Leavis or Winters. His genius lay in the way his mind could leap, in the intuition which could jump from one side to another of the parabola of tradition. Tradition is a key word, for all three of these critics emphasised it heavily in their work; it was, in fact, absolutely central to each of them. Therefore, a somewhat laborious-seeming way of reaching my point may be forgiven when I explain that it was the preface to saying that two of the three had almost no, and Winters had an attenuated, sense of tradition.

I will move rapidly to my justification. Eliot and Leavis scarcely at all, and Winters only in a limited degree, read in and commented upon the poetry of our own day, that is, let us say, post-war poetry. Their tradition stopped short, in practical terms at any rate, though Leavis has approached a justification of this short circuit by implying that the tradition has in fact come to an end. The results of this failure to continue judgement up to and through the most recent poetry have been two. Firstly, detailed criticism has not been brought to bear on the work of poets maturing since the war. Secondly, critics who have applied themselves to contemporary poets (critics of some ability, I mean) have, generally, tried to apply versions of the doctrines of the great preceding critics, or, alternatively, a method derived from the concerns of those critics. As the great men of the previous generation ceased to be concerned with our affairs, so we have been impressed by their mannerisms (seriousness), their preoccupations (morality) and their judgements (the re-elevation of Donne, for example) while we have lost touch with their sense of tradition, because it halted, in its critical operations, so abruptly.

Some concreteness may be given this general view by noting two of the most famous contemporary comments on Lowell. First, Elizabeth Bishop:

'Somehow or other, by fair means or foul, and in the middle of our worst century so far, we have produced a magnificent poet.'

And A. Alvarez:

> '. . . poetry of this order needs neither to be justified nor explained; one should simply be thankful that there is still someone able to write it.'

In so far as either of these statements has any meaning, they represent the two faces of the contemporary critical coin in which Lowell's value is most frequently expressed. Ultimately, their logic may be expressed in two short sentences. Life 'in our time' is such hell that it is remarkable that poetry can be written at all, and, when it happens that by some remarkable effort of will and personal cost someone does write poetry, awe and reverence rather than the application of critical acumen is the appropriate response.

Lest it should be thought that I have selected passages of comment unfairly, other passages may be referred to: Rosenthal's feeling that some passages in *Life Studies* were too private for comment is one; the dust-jackets of Lowell's books are covered with others; the columns of the literary press when a new book appears are full of such references. Gabriel Pearson's study of *For the Union Dead*[4] contains a particularly priceless paragraph:

> 'Lowell's project amounts to making good the claim that literature —with poetry as its most intense manifestation—remains a viable and trustworthy means of shaping and mastering experience. Lowell offers his own literary career (implicitly of course) as the augury and illustration of some possible ultimate cultural good health or good management or at least good luck. He reaffirms the power of literature to order the chaos of society, personality and history, with its own history, its own order, its own virtue. Hence the relief with which each Lowell volume is greeted. The cheers are for fresh news of the survival of literature itself.'

'Augury', 'luck', 'cheers', 'survival'—these are the terms of sorcery and hysteria, not criticism: we are back to Swinburne on Coleridge.

Two observations are worth making at this juncture. First, the 'critical' views quoted above do show the same public concern as Lowell himself; show, indeed, a commitment to the necessity of interaction between literature and society, or public affairs. In its manifestations, however, the commitment is debased, because, as we can see from the quotations, the judging mind has been driven out and replaced by the responses of superstition. None of these remarks taken individually, nor the style of criticism taken as a whole, can say much that is useful or central about poetry. It is therefore ill-equipped to justify the relevance—that is, the public character—of poetry. Being primitively superstitious, rather than morally reasonable, there is no claim on us to take it seriously.

Nonetheless, we ought to do so. This leads me to my second observation. In contemporary criticism and commentary of the kind I have quoted on Lowell, we can see the application of a debased and crude version of the very general testimonies—to life and morality, most notably—that are to be found so strongly in the works of the three critics I have mentioned. There is no doubt about the moral intentions of our literati: certainly they are searching for a comment on life and the quality of poetry as an intense manifestation of it. The debasement is equally evident, however, in a style that uses language to enclose and harmonise a handful of rather primitive emotional reactions: the sense of morality and life in Eliot, Winters and Leavis was demonstrated in the vibrancy and acumen with which they tackled literary texts, in the activity of what I have called the judging mind. Judgement, sustained and serious examinations of texts, set in the comparative context of tradition, is what we now most lack.

The relationship between the quality of the criticism and the quality of the poetry of a given period is, of course, a vexed question. It seems clear enough to me, however, that there is a connection: criticism—and not just literary criticism—is a moral activity, that is, it sets out to make judgements according to certain standards. Curiously, however, codifications of those standards and of the methods of criticism—for example, the codifications of Weller, Richards and others—date quickly. This is because both the standards and the real concerns of criticism are seen only in its practice: like the tradition of literature itself, criticism is a living and changing thing. Nonetheless, its practice is impossible unless there are standards to apply. I assume, in consequence, that good criticism—that is, rational and sensitive criticism—represents the continued existence of good standards in our culture. Such an existence cannot fail to have its effect on poets.

As it happens, this generalisation is given a certain particular substance in the case of Lowell through an account of himself he once gave, in which he referred to the excitement generated in his young life by the imminent appearance of good critical work.

> 'When I was twenty and learning to write, Allen Tate, Eliot, Blackmur, and Winters, and all those people were very much news. You waited for their essays, and when a good critical essay came out it had the excitement of a new imaginative work.' [5]

Lowell is so clearly self-willed and conscientious a poet—as can be shown both from the development of his metres and from the assiduity with which, in his *Imitations*, he tries to draw on the accumulated heritage of literature—that the point about his relationship to the search after value that criticism represents would seem to substantiate itself. But one would not be justified in dealing at such length with criticism of Lowell which one found indifferent in quality and unilluminating in fact were it not that the poet's own work so often strikes the same note as that of his critics—his way of involvement in the life of his time seems so similar to theirs—while an essential characteristic of his work is the way in which he deliberately sets out to reverse that break in critical continuity of which I spoke earlier.

The break in critical continuity is shown in the failure of great critics of recent times fully to carry forward their examination of the tradition into the work of recent poets. Even with Winters, whose master-work, *In Defense of Reason*, contained an extraordinarily brilliant analysis of Wallace Stevens, the short-circuit could be seen, in the brief note on Stevens's last work appended to the main essay in which, in one and a half lines 'The Course of a Particular' was judged 'perhaps the greatest' of Stevens's poems.

The concern, then, was neither carried through nor carried forward. Conversely, with younger critics, the concern is not carried backwards. That is not to say that they do not write—and, indeed, often write well—about the past, but it is as though there was no continuance, as though the subjects were in separate compartments. You rarely feel, when reading a younger critic, that the ordered experiences of a thorough reading, of a lifetime's study of the past, is being brought to bear on the work of a modern poet: you certainly do not get even a hint of this in the comments of any critic that I have read on Lowell; you certainly do not feel very often that a writer praising Lowell is bearing in mind earlier praise given to Donne or Pope—there is no comparative assessment, consequently no tradition, and consequently no just assessment. It is fundamentally in terms of their own feelings about their own time that writers on Lowell judge his work.

Nor is this merely a roundabout way of criticising the critics. Its importance for elucidating the framework of Lowell's own thinking may be shown from two passages:

> At Jehovah's nod
> Satan seemed more let loose amongst us: God
> Abandoned us to Satan, and he pressed
> Us hard, until we thought we could not rest
> Till we had done with life. Content was gone.
> All the good work was quashed. We were undone.
> The breath of God had carried out a planned
> And sensible withdrawal from this land;
> The multitude, once unconcerned with doubt,
> Once neither callous, curious nor devout,
> Jumped at broad noon, as though some peddler groaned
> At it in its familiar twang: 'My friend,
> Cut your own throat. Cut your own throat. Now! Now!'
> September twenty-second, Sir, the bough
> Cracks with the unpicked apples, and at dawn
> The small-mouth bass breaks water, gorged with spawn.
> —*After the Surprising Conversions*

That passage is essentially contemporary: it presents in an elevated

way, against the background of a felt history of religion, a judgement on Lowell's own time and a concern with it: that is the
concern I have called debased in the work of the critics, but it is
the same concern and can be seen more obviously in, for example,
'Central Park', 'Inauguration Day: January 1953', 'Beyond the
Alps' and, of course, 'The Exile's Return'.

The second passage is from 'Falling Asleep over the Aeneid':

> The flaming turkey-feathered arrows swarm
> Beyond the Alps. 'Pallas', I raise my arm
> And shout, 'Brother, eternal health. Farewell
> Forever,' Church is over, and its bell
> Frightens the yellowhammers, as I wake
> And watch the whitecaps wrinkle up the lake.
> Mother's great-aunt, who died when I was eight,
> Stands by our parlour sabre. 'Boy, it's late.
> Vergil must keep the Sabbath.' Eighty years!
> It all comes back. My Uncle Charles appears.
> Blue-capped and bird-like. Phillips, Brooks and Grant
> Are frowning at his coffin, and my aunt,
> Hearing his coloured volunteers parade
> Through Concord, laughs, and tells her English maid
> To clip his yellow nostril hairs, and fold
> His colours on him . . . It is I, I hold
> His sword to keep from falling, for the dust
> On the stuffed birds is breathless, for the bust
> Of young Augustus weighs on Vergil's shelf:
> It scowls into my glasses at itself.

While exhibiting the same involvement in and concern for the
present as the first passage, these lines show another vital aspect of
Lowell: his sense of the contemporaneity of history, of the whole
past. Both these involvements are dramatised in the dramatic
pivot of the poem, the three words 'It is I', words which, following the long perspective already outlined, establish the speaker's
intimate relationship to it—not the old man simply, but all the
men of history have been through these experiences.

But what is this relationship? In my submission Lowell does not
really know. Unquestionably, this failure to penetrate the past is

ultimately a failure of resources, either the non-existence of or the poet's failure to penetrate to a full, complex and subtle range of human values. But I will, if I may, leave this fundamental point for a moment to concentrate on the consequences of Lowell's attempt to fill the vacuum of meaning left by his failure to penetrate the meaning of his own analogies, his failure to distinguish between the different values of different historical episodes and his consequent attempt to concentrate on the whole continuum of historical experience.

First, the vacuum is filled by the wilful violence of Lowell's judgement on his own time. Ultimately—and despite reservations of fondness and admiration for different men and periods—all human experience in history is condemned. Secondly, condemnation as such is not the poet's ambition: that ambition is to find value, to discover the unblemished Adam. But, thirdly, the method adopted—and the attempt to provide an over-mastering analogy for historical episodes and the kaleidoscopic jumbling of persons and periods is a method as well as an achievement—is ultimately destructive.

I now want to return to the fundamental point of the non-existence of resources for judgement or Lowell's failure to penetrate to them. For, as it stands, the meaning of his work is, as Johnson said of 'Lyeidas', uncertain and remote. The break in the continuity of tradition, the failure to judge the present against the past, has had the crude result, not only of a failure to see objectively (as opposed to subjectively) the character of Lowell as a public poet, but also of the simple failure to compare him to other public poets of the past, a proceeding, moreover, surely sanctioned by the *Imitations*.

There are various, more or less complex reasons for the failure to do this, and various, more or less complex, difficulties which the act of the comparison brings up. Just now I want to concentrate on the results of a comparison, from the point of view of the absence of a complex system of value (as opposed to a complex system of reference) in Lowell's work. To this end I insert here a series of passages:

In vain, in vain—the all-composing hour
Resistless falls: the muse obeys the pow'r.
She comes! she comes! the sable throne behold
Of Night primeval and of Chaos old!
Before her, fancy's gilded clouds decay,
And all its varying rainbows die away.
Wit shoots in vain its momentary fires,
The meteor drops, and in a flash expires.
As one by one, at dread Medea's strain
The sick'ning stars fade off th'ethereal plain;
As Argus' eyes by Hermes' wand opprest,
Closed one by one to everlasting rest;
Thus at her felt approach, and secret might,
Art after art goes out, and all is night.
See skulking Truth to her old cavern fled,
Mountains of casuistry heaped o'er her head!
Philosophy, that leaned on heaven before,
Shrinks to her second cause, and is no more.
Physic of metaphysic begs defence,
And metaphysic calls for aid on sense!
See mystery to mathematics fly!
In vain! they gaze, turn giddy, rave, and die
Religion, blushing veils her sacred fires,
And unawares morality expires.
For public flame, nor private, dares to shine,
Nor human spark is left, nor glimpse divine!
Lo! thy dread empire, chaos! is restored;
Light dies before thy uncreating word;
Thy hand, great Anarch! lets the curtains fall
And universal darkness buries all.
                    —Pope, 'The Dunciad', Book IV

Unnumber'd suppliants crowd Preferment's gate,
Athirst for wealth, and burning to be great;
Delusive Fortune hears th' incessant call,
They mount, they shine, evaporate, and fall.
On ev'ry stage the foes of peace attend,
Hate dogs their flight, and insult mocks their end.
Love ends with hope, the sinking statesman's door
Pours in the morning worshipper no more;

For growing names the weekly scribbler lies,
To growing wealth the dedicator flies,
From every room descends the painted face,
That hung the bright Palladium of the place,
And smoak'd in kitchens, or in auctions sold,
To better features yields the frame of gold;
For now no more we trace in ev'ry line
Heroic worth, benevolence divine:
The form distorted justifies the fall,
And detestation rids th' indignant wall.
                    —*Johnson, 'The Vanity of human wishes'*

Turning and turning in the widening gyre
The falcon cannot hear the falconer;
Things fall apart; the centre cannot hold;
Mere anarchy is loosed upon the world,
The blood-dimmed tide is loosed, and everywhere
The ceremony of innocence is drowned;
The best lack all conviction, while the worst
Are full of passionate intensity.

Surely some revelation is at hand;
Surely the Second Coming is at hand.
The Second Coming! Hardly are those words out
When a vast image out of *Spiritus Mundi*
Troubles my sight: somewhere in sands of the desert
A shape with lion body and the head of a man,
A gaze blank and pitiless as the sun,
Is moving its slow thighs, while all about it
Reel shadows of the indignant desert birds.
The darkness drops again; but now I know
That twenty centuries of stony sleep
Were vexed to nightmare by a rocking cradle,
And what rough beast, its hour come round at last,
Slouches towards Bethlehem to be born?
                    —*Yeats, 'The Second Coming'*

On Troy's last day, alas, the populous
Shrines held carnival, and girls and boys
Flung garlands to the wooden horse; so we

2

Burrow into the lion's mouth to die.
Lord, from the lust and dust thy will destroys
Raise an unblemished Adam who will see
The limbs of the tormented chestnut tree
Tingle, and hear the March-winds lift and cry:
'The Lord of Hosts will overshadow us'.
— *Lowell, 'The First Sunday in Lent'*

Each of these extracts represents the tradition of public poetry; in each the poet addresses himself to analysing and assessing the essential quality and characteristics of the life of his time. The material is sought, moreover, not in a study of the way men think, nor in the activity of the imagination, but in what men do, in something which might well be called the outward show or appearance of things. 'The First Sunday in Lent', for example, begins with a sketch of the assembling of people for Sunday service: the whole emphasis of Lowell's moral concern is with public performance. When he examines private moralities he does so after deducing their nature and existence from public attitudes and actions. He continues, always, to judge the quality of private affirmation by reference to public action.

There is, nonetheless, a sharp difference of character between the extracts quoted above, which is to be explained neither by their varying quality nor by the different periods from which they come. In approaching a definition of that difference we must be very much aware (in dealing particularly with Pope) of the tremendously subtle and complex variety of intelligence and imagination displayed by an undoubtedly great poet: this is precisely the variety and complexity of insight which raises such a poet above any period and above any such definition (as, of 'public' poetry) as I have been offering. Moreover, this is a point about the character of Augustan poetry in general and Pope's work in particular that we are still inclined to miss, despite what Dr. Leavis said on the subject more than thirty years ago, in *Revaluation*.

Nonetheless, bearing this warning in mind, there is a crucial and noticeable difference in texture between the extracts quoted.

The variety of condemnation in *The Dunciad* is such that Pope's ease of reference calls to mind the range of virtues supposed to be in decline. In the lines beginning 'Religion, blushing veils her sacred fires' we can see how the placing as well as the use of 'sacred', 'morality', 'flame', 'human' and 'divine' inform us of the immensity of the tragedy involved in the rise of chaos. We are told precisely what it is the poet stands for: more, the authority which Pope claims for his denunciations rests fundamentally on his capacity to define, articulate and press home the value of his own judgement. His is, indeed, a judgement given objective force by the proof presented—in the metre and syntax of his verse—of his capacity to discriminate and evaluate. Compared to this, compared, that is, to this kind of poetry, as well as to Pope's own excellence, 'The First Sunday in Lent' is impoverished. It offers, not only in the stanza quoted but elsewhere, a ringing vigour of denunciation given great force if not great point, by the incantatory beat of the rhythm. But the authority which the poet must claim to make such denunciations is absent because the positive nature of his statement—his definition of the standpoint from which he speaks—is asserted but never described.

Now, it is fashionable—and accurate as far as it goes—to ascribe such a difference in texture to the popularly received judgement that the eighteenth century was a strong civilisation, while ours is a weak one. We have Dr. Leavis's authority for this, and he elaborated the judgement when, writing of Johnson, he said of the strong, positive Augustan tradition that 'the very decided conventions of idiom and form engage comprehensive unanimities regarding morals, society and civilization.' Thus, one might say, words like 'religion', 'sacred' and 'morality' as used by Pope are given particular force in his writing by the place they occupied in the civilisation of his time: their availability, as it were, their received value, free his art and his energy to concentrate on modes of using and presenting them. He can use them; he does not have to explain them.

This simple, forceful and true analysis conceals, however, as many difficulties as it resolves and begs a series of questions. It tells us, for example, little about the real nature of eighteenth-century strength and nothing at all about our own weakness. Conventionally, moreover, the curse which modern writers have to bear (because of the absence in their day of a generally affirmed set of values) is a choice between explaining and justifying each symbol of value in their work and retreating into a world of entirely private symbolism—the choice, that is, between shouldering an intolerable burden of logical argument and retreating into a mindless maze of incommunicable assertions, the choice, in a word, between Joyce and Ginsberg. P. H. Newby, who surveys this dilemma remorselessly in his brilliant novels, wrote about it with great perspicacity just after the war (in a pamphlet entitled *The Novel*), but seems content, in this critical work, with a diagnosis. One of the heroic features of Lowell's work is his refusal to accept or be a victim of the dilemma. Occasionally—and most particularly in *Life Studies*—Lowell uses a symbolism too private, too inexplicable to bear the weight of emphasis he puts on it; he never falls victim to the counter-vice of neurotic over-explanation. A great source of strength has, of course, been his close study of the poetry of other times and languages, which bears fruit in the *Imitations*. The great courage of Lowell, however, is shown in his determination to judge experience, from which he rarely relents, and to judge it—as the whole corpus of his work, particularly in its intricate system of reference to history shows—by objective and immutable rather than contemporary and personal standards. In him the ambition is devised which was natural to the eighteenth century: but it is there and it forms the link with the great tradition of public poetry.

There is always a danger, of course, that this kind of discussion will be invidious where it is not counter-productive. To compare Lowell and Pope against the background of large cultural generalisation and analysis is to invite the simple retort that the comparison of impoverishment with wealth is merely a needlessly complicated way of saying the obvious—that, as a poet, Lowell is much inferior to Pope. That point has to be admitted. Nonetheless, if we remember the pregnant remarks of Eliot (in 'Tradition and the individual talent') about the way in which the process of writing tends to depersonalise writers, because, since the whole line of the tradition is, though perhaps only minutely, altered by each new work, the identity between men who take on the task of creating poetry is more important than the superficial differences time and personality make between them, we may be emboldened to continue.

In any event, it is surely observable, both that Lowell is trying to do something—something, perhaps anterior to the conception of poetry—very like what Pope is doing and that the armoury of Pope's cultural resources for the task in hand is very much richer. It is as though—and this is indeed a crucial point—Lowell is trying to take on himself a burden Pope could share with his civilisation. That undeniable point might well seem, on consideration, to be the strongest mark of a difference between them that defeats useful analogy.

But it is not the whole story, as we can see when we turn to the second of my extracts and Samuel Johnson. Here again we immediately observe both the public character of the poetry and the wide range of virtuous reference—the numerous and subtle categories of good—which Johnson has at his disposal. But we notice, I think, something else as well; we notice, in the most grave, the most traditionally decorous, the most deliberately weighty and epigrammatic of the great Augustan poets, a distinctly personal note—more properly, a note of personality— which is integral to the achievement. If we take the last four lines of the extract quoted we can see the shift that has taken place since Pope and see also the full range of expression and resource of the eighteenth century.

> For now no more we trace in ev'ry line
> Heroic worth, benevolence divine:

Here we have the stately march of Augustan judgement, the pointed and epigrammatic weighing of present experience in the scales against known virtue. The second of these lines, however, is much the more traditionally Augustan, much the more public and impersonal; the first already has a hint of something else—a note of distinct sadness, really—something that is personal to the poet in a way that no line in the quotation from Pope is. It is this note of personality that comes ringing through in the second line of the last couplet:

The form distorted justifies the fall

—this is strong, balanced, justified but conventional.

And detestation rids th' indignant wall

—suddenly we hear struck again a note that we instinctively feel is unique, personal, Johnsonian. Dr. Leavis has spoken of 'the wit that constantly informs the declamatory weight' and the 'constant presence of critical intelligence'[6] but we have, I feel, something more. In 'detestation' and 'indignant' the poet himself steps suddenly forward and puts the weight of his personal feeling behind the judgements of his civilisation. We may feel that Pope's satire, for example, is unique to Pope; but Pope did not exploit his personality, involve and expose himself in the act of judgement, as Johnson did. Here traditional civility and weight and personal impetus combine; here we have, I feel, what Lowell would like to do.

What was working to produce this shift in usage, which Johnson saw and used and Pope did not, though both wrote in an overlapping period? The enduring impact of Johnson comes, of course, neither from his character as an exceptionally forceful representative of his time, nor from the resources of his personality, but from the expression his poetry gives to the strength of his personal faith in the values he represented. Mr. John Sparrow[7] once pointed out how, in criticism, Johnson stood at a cross-road of indecision between an age when the greatness of poetry seemed to be inherent in the subject chosen and one in which it was regarded as inherent in the poet; here was a most important moment in the shift from the classical to the romantic, a moment revealing an impulse crucial to Johnson the poet, which was only half-understood by Johnson the critic. The striking point here, as Mr. Sparrow points out, is the way in which Johnson's intelligence and instinct push him towards a position alien to his strict training and devout traditionalism. Wherein lie the sources of the shift?

The explanation is to be found, I believe, in a passage of truly remarkable insight by Yvor Winters.[8] Summary cannot do justice to the range and complexity of his argument, but it may serve our purpose here. Winters points to the fact that some of Johnson's greatest poetry (notably the prologues to *Comus* and to *A word to the wise*) is 'stereotyped in almost every detail of language' but

> 'are poems of extraordinary power because of the conviction and intelligence of the author, which are expressed mainly in the plot and rational outline, and in a certain tragic irony with which the stereotypes are occasionally used: these poems are the work of a great genius employing a decadent language.'

This is sufficient to throw light and shade on the simple judgement of the eighteenth century as a strong culture, drawing its strength from 'the comprehensive unanimities' of which Dr. Leavis spoke. Rather, Winters suggests elsewhere in the same passages, the language of the eighteenth century, so well established by the middle of the century that men like Johnson were so steeped in it that it dominated their thinking and practice, was itself based on the intellectually unsound and incoherent philosophy of Deism shown at its influential worst in Pope's 'Essay on Man'. The formulae of eighteenth-century judgement ('thinking right and meaning well') were, Winters suggests, sentimental clichés based on naive principles: the deficiency of the age lay in its dependence on them. Unfortunately, the Romantic movement took the show of reason (in the pretty and conventionalised rationalism of the heroic couplet) for the thing itself; assumed the deficiencies of the eighteenth century to be due to excess of reason and themselves abandoned even the pretence of rational thought.

That is, however, to anticipate. My purpose is simply to suggest that, for all its strengths, the tradition and the instrument Johnson had to hand was already conventionalised and in decline and that, instinctively, he had recourse to the weight of his personality and conviction to shore it up. By Lowell's time the exposure involved in that procedure is intense, but the proceeding is nonetheless the same, the use of the poet's personality as an instrument of judgement: of that procedure Johnson was the great originator.

When we compare Lowell to Yeats we are within a narrower time span. Again, in 'The Second Coming' the public ambition is the same; what has vanished altogether is any complex system of moral reference such as Pope and Johnson had for use. Every word in this poem, from the characteristically esoteric and egotistic formula with which it opens is, however, stamped with the ineradicable mark of Yeats's personality. We can feel the tight authority in his irony

> The best lack all conviction, while the worst
> Are full of passionate intensity.

Here, however, the framework of moral reference is secular: 'conviction' and 'passionate' are used as 'flame' is in the lines from *The Dunciad* examined above; no attempt is made to invest them with the historical significance of 'religion', 'morality' and 'sacred' in Pope; they did not enjoy such civilisational sanction. The obvious weight of this couplet—its irony—lies, however, in the transference of the epithet, passionate applied to 'worst' rather than 'best'. We sense this irony only imperfectly, however, —we sense it from the way the words are arranged—if we do not know our Yeats. For the word is given extra weight by the definitions of it elaborated elsewhere in the poet's work. 'Passionate', for Yeats represented a quite extraordinary weight of moral conviction which was worked out and justified in detail in his theoretical writings as well as in his poetry. If we know the work well, our appreciation of the weight given to 'passionate' in this poem will be enriched; but Yeats's use of the word in any event enjoys impact because his own studies and theoretical formulations gave confidence and stability to his use of it and we sense this.

Of course it is undeniable that the weight of Yeats's authority depends on a carefully elaborated private structure of meaning and symbolism carefully explained to the public. This is itself a deficient procedure, since it compels the poet to be priest, prophet and philosopher, as well as poet; it inhibits the tradition (Yeats has, so far, enjoyed too little direct influence) because one man's self-created structure is unlikely to become the poetic religion of another; and even at its best the poetry may be esoteric or obscure.

In a small but not insignificant example of this, I take the word 'mere' in the fourth line of 'The Second Coming' to enjoy there its original Latin meaning (from the adjective 'merus' or 'pure' or 'unadulterated'). (It is thus used particularly in Horace, where it is applied to wine.) 'Pure' itself—though it might superficially appear to enjoy the same attraction as the transferred 'passionate' —would not do in place of 'mere', because its connotations of delicacy would break up the force of the phrase. Mere is exactly the right word in this place.

Nonetheless, if the reader takes the more conventional meaning of mere, as, that is, solely what the noun implies (one example given in the OED is 'merest buffoonery'), with a slighting or contemptuous overtone, the force of the passage is weakened. True, a slighting reference is tolerable in the first stanza because Yeats is speaking there authoritatively: nonetheless it would be out of balance with the scale of the next four lines. I suspect, however, that most readers take the word in its slighting sense and pass over the weakness this entails in the structure with no more than puzzlement because the eccentricity involved is drowned in the atmosphere of mystery and significance in which the poem is enveloped. I cannot, of course, prove that Yeats meant the word in the sense in which I prefer to use it. I simply argue that it makes better poetry that way. I maintain also that its weight and importance may well be missed, because of Yeats's method and this likelihood (many more important examples could be cited, and the same process is at work in the minds of many critics who have failed to appreciate the full significance of 'passionate' as well as, very widely, in writings on Yeats which fail to understand his

2*

use of Irish idiom) is not only characteristic, but diminishes the poetry.

Yeats wrote as early as 1892 that a Poet Laureate should be fully responsible to the nation alone 'to celebrate matters of national importance ... the deaths of famous men of thought and action, and the ever-coming never-coming light of that ideal peace and freedom where to all nations are staggering in the darkness'; Mr. Thomas Parkinson has written of his life-long struggle to develop 'the unshaped image of reborn Ireland'; there is no doubt about his character as a public poet. At the same time he was an intensely personal one. 'Under Ben Bulben', his testimony to his successors, underlines the extent to which he saw himself and his personality as central to his public task; that work could best be performed, he once wrote, by writing 'out our own thoughts in as nearly as possible the language we thought them in ... for our lives give them force ...'. It may well have been his direct involvement in the life of his country that saved Yeats from what might otherwise have been the degenerate obscurity of his philosophical doctrines.

It is, perhaps, the unfamiliar concept of personal and public that Yeats represented—developed as a doctrine and not simply carried on as a practice—combined with the mystical character of his theories and the unfamiliarity of his idioms that has forced him into the curiously ambiguous position he now occupies in English literary criticism. Both Winters and Leavis speak of him disparagingly and both give as part of their reason the fact that they find the evidence for sustaining the violence of his feelings— that is, the evidence provided by his network of private symbolism—inadequate. Yet, aside from my judgement of his greatness, I feel the failure to make Yeats central to the modern study of our literature a great loss, because he grappled so manfully with and to such a great extent overcame that tremendous dilemma of taking a public burden on a private personality which is so endemic to Lowell and his writing.

It must by now be clear that, in contrasting Yeats with Lowell, I am contrasting what I take to be success with what I take to be (relatively) failure. The question nonetheless remains: how do these two nearly contemporary poets go about a job very similarly conceived, while beset by a very similar problem involved in the decline of the moral authority of both language and its supporting concepts? Yeats, I have suggested, was very greatly helped by the kind of involvement he had with emerging Ireland; he was also endowed (as Mr. Sparrow pointed out in the lecture already quoted, commenting on 'Cold Heaven' and 'A Dialogue of Self and Soul') with a remarkable richness of personality and nature. Indeed, Mr. Sparrow believes that therein lay the essence of his greatness. His endeavour, however, also took another direction, that of cultivating and developing poetic form. He sought a 'passionate objectivity' of utterance and felt that this could essentially be achieved only through the development of the 'syntax' of his poetry. He clearly believed that the right form could lend authority to his statement and the incantatory form he achieved in his late work was the pinnacle of that stylistic achievement.

The same conviction and predisposition is evident in Lowell. In his early work the formality and complexity of his technique were much remarked upon and, when it was loosened and relaxed, other forces (which I will discuss later) were at work. The climax of this early preoccupation came in 'Thanksgiving's over'. In this, as in the rest of the earlier work, Lowell uses form deliberately, as a separate instrument from perception, for refining and moulding his experience. 'Thanksgiving's over' has an almost incredibly complex metrical structure and an unintelligible pattern of religious symbolism. Eight years later the whole edifice was abandoned for the informality of *Life Studies*.

The preoccupation with form seems to me to represent the search for authority in poetry at a very deep level. It recalls the fact that, in his later poetry, Yeats took the subject of and the possibility of writing well as material in itself; such was the life-long preoccupation of Wallace Stevens, which led his admirer, Professor Frank Kermode, to hazard the guess that, at a very deep level, the subject of all good poetry was the writing of (or the possibility of writing) good poetry; and this concern is, of course, the source of Mr. Gabriel Pearson's remark quoted earlier, that the appearance of a Lowell volume was a testimony to the continued possibilities of writing. This last is, of course, a highly superficial view of a complex phenomenon. For whatever cause, language and the concepts of moral value it enshrines, no longer provide sustenance sufficient for authoritative poetry. The act of attempting to write such poetry of course betrays a faith that this can be done: it is in consequence natural to try to search out the resources of authority in the poetry itself, that is, in form. But, of course, this can never be a self-sufficient process, and it is a tribute to Lowell's courage that he abandoned it at the point where, in 'Thanksgiving's over', his almost exclusive concern with form was becoming corrupting.

It was also about this point that Lowell abandoned religion as the source of an independent system of moral reference and evaluation to put against quotidian experience in his verse. The trouble with his religious structure was, of course, precisely its failure to provide him with—or his failure to find in it—a wide and flexible system of values. His theology (his New England theology) was always very Puritanical; it was also inhuman. The message was that it was wrong to go on as we were going, but no suggestion was offered that to do differently would make us happier, even in an afterlife. There was here the danger of a rather frantic aristocratic disdain for life. It was not suggested that even the 'unblemished Adam' could achieve happiness.

What sustained this vision, the incomplete conceptual character of which was shown in the Virgin Mary passages in 'The Quaker Graveyard', was the frequent felicity of expression, the rhythm of the whole and the internal logic of the condemnation: the trophies of childhood in 'The First Sunday in Lent', when rigorously examined, warrant the conclusion which is sustained rather than impaired by the alteration in time and pace of the poem based on the (acceptable) transition from childhood to adulthood. But the poem cannot bear the full weight of its apocalyptic conclusion both because the human faults it describes are not rooted in human variety, and are not, anyway, sufficiently important faults to sustain the grandeur of the conclusion. There is no flexibility, no range of sin and error in Lowell's catechism: all fault warrants the ultimate condemnation. He seeks to judge nature from conduct, finds all conduct sinful and therefore all nature repellent.

This disease of sensibility in New England writing Yvor Winters called 'Maule's Curse', from Matthew Maule's prophecy that New England Puritans would drink their own blood because the theology they adopted—the predestinarian theology that dubbed all fault mortal in the eyes of the Lord, demanded apocalyptic repentence from all sinners and at the same time maintained the inability to repent and the inefficacy of repentance— was profoundly alien to human nature.[9] Maule's curse is the most formidable evidence of his New England heritage in Robert Lowell. It was, of course, profoundly alien to the supposedly Catholic theology of his earlier work; in forcing New England Puritanism into a Catholic mould Lowell rigidified both; after 'Thanksgiving's over', in order to continue writing, he had to abandon doctrines that threatened to swallow him up.

The inadequacy of both poetic forms and religion as life systems left Lowell with only New England and, in a wider sense, America, as subjects. In small domestic poems (notably in *For the Union Dead*) and in wry moments of affection for his ancestors, Lowell achieved a certain balance, a momentary tranquillity. But fundamentally, perhaps because he was still struggling to free himself from its theology, he found more to hate than to love in his own history. New England and his hate threatened also to swallow him up, because his own attitude of total condemnation was as inhuman as what he was attacking, his own total condemnation of the self-righteousness leading to injustice of historical New England culture was ultimately destructive.

Lowell was left with himself, with the richness or poverty of his own nature and personality, which he lacerated in search of truth in *Life Studies*. This unrelieved focus—of, say, 'Skunk Hour'— could not long be maintained without madness. Lowell was left with two resources. One was the private and obscure world of historical analogy of 'Falling Asleep over the Aeneid': but this is always ultimately incomplete and unsatisfactory because, as Holloway pointed out, we can only see that there is some analogy, not what it is. Nevertheless, though flawed, work in this vein is impressive, if neither wholly satisfactory nor commensurate in achievement with Lowell's ambition. The other resource was the *Imitations*, the one mode of work which has remained constant throughout Lowell's development. If only because they are so consistent a resource for the poet, I believe the *Imitations* have been insufficiently attended to. Although, moreover, they manifest many of the same general problems discussed elsewhere in this chapter, they have, in relation both to Lowell and to the tradition, special features and promises which raise large general questions more appropriate for discussion in a conclusion than in an introduction, and to my conclusion I have reserved them.

I have described what seem to me to be the general features—and the general implications and results—of Lowell's poetic impulse. I have also tried to place this discussion in the framework of the appropriate poetic tradition and I hope that I will be able to sustain the points I have made in later chapters. Much is, if not speculation, at least argument not susceptible to arithmetical proof. That seems to me, however, to be a lesser danger than the danger of erecting formulations of the tradition which are too exclusive. I may have left myself open to that charge by excluding from this introduction all discussion of what used to be thought of as the modern movement in poetry—that of Pound and Eliot.

To include them, however, would seem to me to make this book something other than it is intended to be—a study of Robert Lowell the public poet. Ultimately the tradition of English poetry is indivisible but, within the English tradition since Shakespeare, there have been two distinct lines, what Leavis calls the line of wit, running from Shakespeare and Jonson through the Metaphysicals and changing into the cultivation of sensibility of the Romantics, and what I have called public poetry—or the line of gravity—running from Shakespeare (the statecraft of the plays is the great example) through Pope (who was also a Metaphysical—the lines had not yet diverged), Johnson and Yeats to Lowell. Embarking on his own poetic career Eliot detected an affinity of impulse between himself and the Metaphysical poets. That affinity manifested itself in a poetry apparently quite different from Donne's but with the same underlying character and concerns. I am now suggesting another such identification—though it is late in the day to make detections—and I have chosen Samuel Johnson as the pivotal figure because with him we see the unwilling introduction of the personal responsibility of the poet into the tradition of public poetry; that introduction was, as I hope to show, neurotic as well as individual, as is the poetry of Lowell.

One final point. Shakespeare is clearly the fount of the development, the instigator of the tradition. A passage from *Richard II* suggests why. In John of Gaunt's speech in II.i. we find

> Methinks I am a prophet new inspired
> And thus expiring do foretell of him:
> His rash fierce blaze of riot cannot last,
> For violent fires soon burn out themselves;
> Small showers last long, but sudden storms are short;

The measured gravity of this, leading as it does to the famous patriotic passage on England, recalls Johnson's firework's image, 'They mount, they shine, evaporate, and fall.' In the same speech, however, we are given the embryonic essence of metaphysical wit, the play upon words that overturns and analyses reality:

> He tires betimes that spurs too fast betimes;
> With eager feeding food doth choke the feeder:
> Light vanity, insatiate cormorant,
> Consuming wears, soon preys upon itself,

And to both of these is added the solvent of Johnson's personality, which fuses the two together in pursuit of a high theme: that personality is the equivalent of the poet's personal responsibility we have been discussing. This is also very public poetry; it recalls Johnson's injunction, now too readily ignored, that a great subject is essential for great poetry and that blank verse (and perhaps modern free verse?) is impossible without it. Certainly it is true that no mind since Shakespeare's could contain within

itself the creation of these two lines of development, of philosophical wit and public gravity. It is consequently not surprising
that poets since have developed one or other of the lines. In our
time poets have gone back for inspiration, not to Shakespeare,
but to one of his subsidiary lines. If I am right we ought to go
back to another subsidiary. If that is the case, if the self propulsion
of the lines of development from Shakespeare has stopped, if we
must feed back to go on, then the conclusion of much of the
speculation in this introduction must be that, whatever the
reasons, the tradition—the Shakespeare dominated tradition—
has come to an end; unless yet more can be found in Shakespeare;
or another Shakespeare arises.

IN 1944 LOWELL published his first volume, *Land of Unlikeness*.
It was followed in 1946 by *Lord Weary's Castle* and, in 1951, by
The Mills of the Kavanaughs. In 1950 his first volume was published in England. Entitled *Poems 1938–49*, it contained seven
poems from his first volume, the entire contents of the second and
all but the title poem of the third. This last was, however, included
in the first edition in England of *Robert Lowell: the First Twenty
Years*, by Hugh B. Staples, in 1962. *Poems 1938–49* therefore contains the great bulk of Lowell's writing in the first phase of his
career. He revises relatively little and (unlike, say, Graves) dis-
misses work from the canon rarely. One or two revisions of
importance will be treated in succeeding pages and chapters but,
for a bibliographically definitive account of Lowell's first phase,
one cannot do better than turn to Mr. Staples's volume. In almost
all circumstances, however, and for the convenience of the British
reader, I will refer to *Poems 1938–49*. This volume, with one
exception, provides the material for the analysis in this chapter;
the exception is 'The Quaker Graveyard in Nantucket' which,
with the poem, 'The Mills of the Kavanaughs' is examined in
Chapter Three, as representing Lowell's most deliberate and
sustained attempts at long poems. I have not thought it necessary
to provide comprehensive bibliographical references, a proceeding
which would be an adumbration where it was not merely a
repetition, of Mr. Staples's work.

    The first seventy pages of the English edition of *Poems 1938–49*
contain work largely from *Lord Weary's Castle*, but including
six poems—'In Memory of Arthur Winslow', 'Concord',
'Salem', 'Children of Light', 'The Drunken Fisherman',
'Napoleon crosses the Beresina'—from *Land of Unlikeness*. None
of the six, however, went directly from *Land of Unlikeness* to
Poems; all appeared in revised versions in *Lord Weary's Castle*;

while the *Land of Unlikeness* versions of 'Salem', 'Concord', and 'Dea Roma', were themselves revisions of versions appearing still earlier in periodical publications. Finally, the poem 'Death from Cancer on Easter' in *Land of Unlikeness* became (as 'Death from Cancer') Part One of the revised version of another *Land of Unlikeness* poem, 'In Memory of Arthur Winslow', in *Lord Weary's Castle*.

The history of these poems, combined with their placing in *Poems*, conceals (for all the convenience of that volume) the development of Lowell through his first three volumes—*Land of Unlikeness*, *Lord Weary's Castle* and *The Mills of the Kavanaughs*. Except, however, at the very end, in 'Thanksgiving's Over', that development is neither fundamental nor revolutionary: in 'Thanksgiving's Over', an incomprehensible poem, lacking rational content, but possessing, nonetheless, a highly intricate and coherent metrical structure, the early Lowell becomes corrupt. (The same is true to a large extent, of the long poem 'The Mills of the Kavanaughs'.)

What is striking, however, about Lowell's development through the first three volumes is, firstly, the perfection of form, noted from the very beginning (and pointed up by Allen Tate in his introduction to *Land of Unlikeness*) and, secondly, the way in which the three volumes (and the work assembled in *Poems*) reveal all the preoccupations of Lowell's career, religion, New England, history, politics and private psychology. *Lord Weary's Castle* shows an advance over *Land of Unlikeness* in confidence, and in the assurance of Lowell's handling of his ideas, while *The Mills of the Kavanaughs* demonstrates the break-up of the moral and intellectual order of Lowell's poetry which was fully revealed in *Life Studies*. That break-up was accompanied by further complexities in his use of metre, by an ever more complicated and convoluted marriage between metrical form and private religious symbolism.

Even at his best, that is, when his work echoes with meaning and reverberation—as in 'Falling Asleep over the Aeneid'—there is a deficiency in the rational content of Lowell's work, which I have attributed to the clash between his search for the platform from which to make an authoritative statement and the defensive ambiguity into which his failure to discover resources for judgement tempts him. *Land of Unlikeness* was his most apocalyptic collection; *Lord Weary's Castle* showed, in some respects (and particularly in 'In the Cage') a slight shift towards the principle of seeking the resources of judgement in the recesses of his own personality; 'Thanksgiving's Over' is a final desperate attempt to make the older preoccupations, with apocalypse and form, work. On its failure, Lowell changed course. In all the shifts of mood and emphasis in the first phase of his career, therefore, Lowell constantly exhibited certain characteristics, the personal violence and the public ambition discussed in the last chapter and an underlying and stubborn concern with, and technical mastery of, metrical form; that concern was, indeed (and here lay many of his deficiencies) independent of rational content or cultural resource; it was an over developed tool, functioning independently of his main task but, ultimately, the final resource on which he called for authority to make pronouncements, the final and most obvious proof that he actually was a poet.

All the preoccupations of Lowell are, therefore, laid out in *Poems 1938-49*. Two features of the order of priority in which they appear must, however, be stressed. The first is that the dominating concern in the volume is the ambition to pronounce a judgement on the ways of men. The second is that the overmastering stamp of religious preoccupation is everywhere in evidence. New England becomes an example of the historical corruption of man— one which possesses a particular obsessive fascination for Lowell— but not a formative—or not avowedly so—influence on him. It is later, in *Life Studies*, that he tries to explain and use the influence of his heritage upon himself: there he maintains his essential judgement but acknowledges a potent influence, this acknowledgement becomes even more open (and therefore more potent) in *For the Union Dead*:

> Father, forgive me
> my injuries,
> as I forgive

those I
have injured!

You never climbed
Mount Sion, yet left
dinosaur
death-steps on the crust,
where I must walk.

—Middle Age

The significance of this argument about dominating concerns
and priorities is best explained fully by examining some texts.
Before doing this, however, it may be helpful to note simply the
way in which style and preoccupation shifted through the first
three volumes (excepting again, for later examination, the two
long poems). The twenty-one poems of *Land of Unlikeness* were
vatic in character and intensity; the overall concern was with
human alienation from God and the note struck was almost
exclusively religious. In *Lord Weary's Castle*, the religious concern
remained dominant, but it was now less vatic and, in some poems,
though it ultimately asserted control, it nonetheless often appeared
to take the form of a sub-theme. The world of Lord Weary was
recognisably contemporary: human sins and cruelties rather than
apocalyptic allegories made up the formulae of the verse. Themes
were introduced from secular (and particularly classical) history
and from personal and ancestral history and some of the religious
experience was transmuted into mysticism rather than apocalypse.
During this stage of development certain techniques—juxtaposition of symbols, transitions (which I will explain below), narrative,
and monologue were worked out and these were packed with an
even greater profusion than ever before of religious forms and
symbolisms into *The Mills of the Kavanaughs*.

The dominating feature of 'In Memory of Arthur Winslow' is,
as Staples puts it (without emphasising the importance of his
insight) the way in which 'the sordidness of the present vitiates
even the nobility of the past.' This is not, indeed, precisely what
happens in the poem, but it does give a good indication of what
is going on. The real difficulty—the real weakness—is that, in his

judgement of New England history, Lowell is essentially using the same technique of judgement that he condemns in his ancestors: this is Maule's curse with a vengeance.

I want to take 'Arthur Winslow' (the revised version in *Poems*) and examine it, first from the point of view of rational coherence and meaning, then as a poem. I shall try to explain why these two points seem to me to be intricately and vitally related.

'In Memory of Arthur Winslow' is an elegy for Lowell's grandfather. The first section, consisting of two stanzas entitled 'Death from Cancer', describe Winslow's death. In the private section of Massachusetts Hospital—Phillys House—we find Winslow dying—'wrestling with the crab'. We are told that Charon—who ferries the souls of the dead across the Styx—will end Winslow's struggle with his disease, but the implication—conveyed by the symbolism of Charon—is that this will not be by way of final death, but as the preface to an after-life. We thus have the principle of an after-life smoothly and almost unnoticeably established as part of the poem's system of reference in the first stanza. Charon is, however, described as a longshoreman, and this description eases Lowell's way—through an entirely acceptable reference to Winslow's state of mind before death—to a description of activity outside the hospital, in Boston Basin, and his grandfather's reaction to it. Winslow is made to wonder

> why the coxes' squeakings dwarf
> The *resurrexit dominus* of all the bells.

Thus, in his final moments of life, the heightened perception which the imminence of death brings, causes Winslow to wonder at something which—as the rest of the poem establishes—the materialism of his life concealed from him before, the contemporary domination of secular concern over religious insight.

Both rationally and poetically this stanza seems to me almost entirely successful. The purist might quarrel a little with the elaboration of the cancer image:

> The claws drop flesh upon your yachting blouse

but 'crab' and this line reinforce the horror of cancer (supposedly a peculiarly contemporary disease) and prepare the introduction of Charon. Later the quiet verb 'ponder', after the active and imagistic 'wrestling', 'drop', 'stab', 'crush' introduces exactly the hush of approaching death which skims upwards

> shells
> Hit water by the Union Boat Club wharf:
> You ponder why the coxes' squeakings dwarf
> The *resurrexit dominus* of all the bells.

'Ponder', therefore, occupies a unique position in the structure of the stanza. It is preceded mainly by active verbs deriving from the sound of 'wrestling' (there is an inner contrast, as between the drawn out struggle for life and the sudden completeness of death, between 'wrestling' and 'stab') and followed by two contrasting themes of sound and meaning 'squeakings' for secular life and the last line for the life of the soul. Internally, within the last couplet (apart altogether from the support given by the already established theme of life after death) the moral predominance of religion is established by the fact that the two appelations ('squeakings' to the coxes and '*resurrexit dominus*' to the bells) are, each within their line entirely appropriate as descriptions: it is in the contrast between the two lines that the triumphant religious assertion drives itself home. The assertion is made more arresting as well as more complex by the irony in 'dwarf', a surprising and not wholly satisfactory usage which, however, is rhythmically prepared for by 'wharf' and partially sustained by its introduction of a new perspective, in that it is a word of size, while the words it brings into relation with one another are words of sound.

It is impossible entirely satisfactorily to explain the effect of rhythm and poetic reverberation on the human sensibility. Suffice it to say that complexities of rhythm and exact meaning which we find in this stanza quite closely reflect a part of the way in which human impulses and emotions work. In life, however, these impulses and emotions are partly controlled by human rationality. In the poem (in *this* poem) the implications of overall

meaning conveyed by the local (or dictionary) meaning and
sounds of the words used are sustained by the rational coherence
of the two statements in the stanza—that there is a life after death
and, hence, the possibility of judging performance in this life and
that, near death, a man ponders why a more important life theme
should be subdued by a lesser in this life. There is, of course, a
cycle here, in that the poetic effects sustain the rational statements
as well and, indeed, give them their authority. What, in effect, the
poet is saying is that, in ordinary secular life, there is a range of
infinitely complex moral meaning (conveyed in the complexity
of the poetic statement) which ought to be examined against the
(poetically justified) statements that there is an after-life and that,
nonetheless, man has allowed quotidian existence to dominate
what ought to be his preparation for it.

We have, then, a stage well-nigh perfectly set. The second
stanza, however, offers no development. The physical description
of Boston is expanded; the social *milieu* of Winslow has been
desecrated

> where with tub
> And strainer the mid-Sunday Irish scare
> The sun-struck shallows for the dusky chub

True, the assertion of after-life is, in this stanza, given a
particularly Christian formulation:

> the ghost
> Of risen Jesus walks the waves to run
> Arthur upon a trumpeting black swan
> Beyond Charles River to the Acheron

The second stanza, then, offers merely notes on the first. The
argument is taken no farther. In particular the contemporary
antithesis between religion and materialism, defined, remains
unexplored. The act of definition, precise though it is, is a minor
achievement. There is a certain amount of conviction carried by
the assonance of the first stanza, but it is introductory conviction.
It is filled out but not increased in weight by the second stanza.

Part II—'Dunbarton'—describes the funeral of Winslow and introduces the historical New England background. The first six lines describe the family cemetery at Dunbarton. It is visualised as waiting:

> The granite plot and the dwarf pines are green
> From watching for the day
> When the great year of the little yeomen come
> Bringing its landed Promise and the faith
> That made the Pilgrim Makers take a lathe
> And point their wooden steeples lest the Word be dumb.

A new scene is set here, in sound but conventional verse. Lowell has turned over the coin to let us see the other side. The coin is that showing materialism rising above religion, now in the particular locale of historical New England. The point is neatly, if rather over-subtly made, by the re-introduction of the word 'dwarf' in line five. Here, in the first stanza of part three, it is suggested (by 'dwarf') that the historical New England of the Starks and Winslows—under pressure from the Irish in the second stanza of Part I—are themselves corrupt. Still, they themselves, though dead, expect a kind of (secular?—the point is unclear) resurrection, coming from the realisation of the promise, their faith in which they tried to implement by spreading the Word of God in the New World.

The second stanza of Part II denies the hope of the dead.

> O fearful witnesses, your day is done:
> The minister from Boston waves your shades,
> Like children, out of sight and out of mind.

The promise, then, is not fulfilled. How the minister from Boston killed it is recorded in the last three lines:

> The preacher's mouthings still
> Deafen my poor relations on the hill:
> Their sunken landmarks echo what our fathers preached.

The 'poor relations' are, of course, those buried in the family cemetery; their gravestones are the sunken and now unconvincing or inadequate statements of what the dead had once preached. An unresolved ambiguity enters with these lines. The preacher's words are dismissed as 'mouthings', clearly by the poet, speaking, not without sympathy, for the Winslow dead. Is it 'mouthings' that enables him to wave the shades away? Is it, that is, that modern Boston is insensitive to the values of old Boston? Or is it that the failure of the 'landmarks' to get across their message to today represents some weakness in the original preachings of the fathers whom they represent?

This is a point of real substance. The graveyard scene is depicted with gravity and decorum. Its physical details are noted precisely and effectively. The contrast in appearances between the past and today is twice vividly noted as modern motor-cars enter and leave the country peace at the funeral of Winslow. In the first stanza

> The stones are yellow and the grass is gray
> Past Concord and the rotten lake and hill
> Where crutch and trumpet meet the limousine

And in the second the decorum of the funeral itself is interrupted:

> The first selectman of Dunbarton spreads
> Wreaths of New Hampshire pine cones on the lined
> Casket where the cold sun
> Is melting. But, at last, the end is reached;
> We start our cars.

This is very well and sensitively done. It can be given serious weight, however, only by a decision in the last three lines that directs our interpretation of what went before. These lines being ambiguous and uncharged the description remains affecting but conventional. We have seen development on one of the basic themes, however, if not decision. A question has been gently posed as to whether yesterday or today is to be held responsible for the contemporary upheaval of values, articulated in the light of the proposition that there is an after-life. The introduction is, as it were, given a new twist. One unsustained note of personal intervention by the poet has been struck—in 'mouthings'—but that might be allowed to pass by his authority as a reporter of the graveside scene.

In Part III—'Five Years Later'—another aspect of the first stanza of Part I is turned over. In Part I Winslow 'pondered' the dwarfing of the bells by the coxes' squeaking: he knew there was something wrong with this state of affairs but did not penetrate its full meaning. In Part III the poet comes forward in uncompromising judgement on the activities of his grandfather:

> I came to mourn you, not praise the craft
> That netted you a million dollars,

The tone here clearly condemns the activity of becoming rich. In the second half of the first stanza, however, Lowell claims to demonstrate, not only that the activity of money-making is itself corrupt, but that the effects of the corruption into which his grandfather fell can be seen in the poet's own time:

> Leaving Columbus in Ohio, shell
> On shell of our stark culture strikes the sun
> To fill my head with all our fathers won
> When Cotton Mather wrestled with the fiends from hell.

The judgement has by now been greatly expanded. Essentially these four lines accuse New England of hypocrisy: while Cotton Mather imagined he was wrestling with the fiends of hell, he was in fact preparing the way for today's stark culture. Lowell himself now grasps the poverty of the heritage of his fathers. New England's priorities were wrong from the beginning and the ambiguity of the last three lines of the second stanza in Part II is in large part resolved. The reader may be allowed to note, however, that the culpability of the past is neither poetically nor rationally established. It is supported merely by a juxtaposition between Lowell's account of his grandfather's activities and the 'stark

culture', visible evidence of which is seen in the landscape out
from Columbus, Ohio.[1] This device of juxtaposition is very common to Romantic poetry since Wordsworth; it is to be found
throughout modern poetry, and particularly in Eliot: see the
contrast between Section IV and Sections II and V of *The Waste
Land* and particularly the famous passage where Eliot contrasts
closing time in a pub with a rich passage from Shakespeare, thus
creating an instrument of judgement from Shakespeare's lines:

> HURRY UP PLEASE ITS TIME
> Goonight Bill. Goonight Lou. Goonight May. Goonight
> Ta ta. Goonight. Goonight.
> Goodnight, ladies, goodnight, sweet ladies, goodnight,
>   Goodnight.

I do not want to go into Eliot's practice here (it seems to me to
be in many ways deficient) but merely to suggest the widespread
use of the juxtapositional device. Its use in 'Arthur Winslow' is
crucial because it occurs at the point where Lowell is stepping
over from mere description (as far as it goes, acceptable) of the
corruption of his grandfather, to a much larger judgement, one
spelling out the taint from the beginning of New England society,
which is even more clearly articulated in Part IV ('A Prayer for
my grandfather to Our Lady'):

> Mother, for these three hundred years or more
> Neither our clippers nor our slavers reached
> The haven of your peace in this Bay State:
> Neither my father nor his father.

The means—and the quality of the means—Lowell uses to convey
this judgement are obviously of vital importance: so weighty a
judgement cannot rest on mere assertion.

I want, therefore, to contrast Lowell's use of the device with an
entirely successful use, by Wordsworth (which is also the example
chosen by Mr. Brooks). Part of 'She dwelt among the untrodden
ways' reads

> A maid whom there were none to praise
> And very few to love
> A violet by a mossy stone
> Half-hidden from the eye!
> —Fair as a star, when only one
> Is shining in the sky.

These juxtapositions are set down very barely. Their meaning may be (and has been to many critics) obscure at first sight. That meaning is, simply, that, though, like a simple violet, Lucy and her qualities are hidden from the great world, to her lover she is as resplendent and unique as Venus. (Authority for this statement is easily established by the convention of a lover's blindness.) The contrast between Lucy's public insignificance and her importance to her lover is the theme of the poem. This idea is large in itself, but its impact is essentially conveyed by the purity of the diction, surrounding as this does the intimate juxtaposition of the contrasts. That intimacy—like the touching of two live electric wires —is achieved by the paring away of the logical prose structure that could have amplified the logical (or prose) meaning of the contrasts. The juxtaposition creates the poetry of the whole, though our eye should not be allowed to slip from the convention of lover's insight on which the whole structure rests.

Paring away logical supports of course creates obscurity. This merits a note. In the best passages of Shakespeare, obscurity, when it exists, is created by an overcrowding of positive intellectual impulses. It is the result of—as Harding said of Rosenberg— bringing 'language to bear on the incipient thought at an earlier stage of its development'. It is the compression of highly specific and concrete images. That compression is what, at root, we mean by poetic. Though the casual eye may see a similarity, in Wordsworth's usage the phenomenon is entirely different. Shakespeare achieved his poetic effect positively—almost by having too much to put in. Wordsworth achieves his negatively, by taking things out, in this case the logical structure supporting the argument.

The achievement (which is small) of the poem quoted remains, though our realisation of how it was done diminishes the value we give it. That negative action may lead to inexplicable obscurity. It may be a sign of decadence. Its cultivation in modern writing is, of course, headlong. The practice was effectively described by Hemingway: 'The story was about coming back from the war, but there was no mention of the war in it'. In other words—as Hemingway said elsewhere in *A Moveable Feast*—the practice consists in finding what you can leave out while retaining—or perhaps thereby increasing—impact.

These notes on the history of the device of juxtaposition illuminate Lowell's argument and method in Part III of 'Arthur Winslow'. Here there is neither compression nor obscurity: there is merely an assertion conveyed by juxtaposition. The *appearance* of this assertion is uniquely conveyed in the lines 'Hosing out gold in Colorado's waste' and 'shell on shell of our stark culture'. Its meaning can be reduced quite easily to prose, and rather neurotic prose at that: 'My grandfather spent much of his time making money. This concealed from him the real spiritual dilemma of our time. We have a rotten culture, the nature of which can be seen in its stark appearance. This is, however, due as much to the mistaken priorities of our common ancestors as to my grandfather'. The poetry adds nothing of significance to this statement and the prose has at least the merit of simplicity. It is a simplicity, moreover, that reveals Lowell's crucial stanza as assertion rather than authority.

For a moment, in the second stanza of Part III Lowell appears to veer. He lists the outward appearances of Winslow's family's greatness and considers for a moment the possibility that his grandfather might have meant well by his pursuit of gold. This is, however, a note of elegiac kindness, for Lowell makes quite clear his view that the pursuit of money is itself an evil activity:

> for what else could bring
> You, Arthur, to the veined and alien West
> But devil's notions that your gold at least
> Could give back life to men who whipped or
> backed the King?

On this note of New England history—in this revised version
of which Lowell maintains that there was no difference of quality
between rebels and loyalists in the War of Independence—Lowell
turns to Part IV and his condemnation of three hundred years of
history already quoted. These two stanzas—with, in the second,
a repeated condemnation of Winslow's failure to penetrate the
real meaning of religion

>   the door
>   To Trinity, the costly Church,

contain Lowell's plea for rescue to the Virgin Mary:

> O Mother, I implore
> Your scorched, blue thunderbreasts of love to pour
> Buckets of blessings on my burning head
> Until I rise like Lazarus from the dead:
> *Lavabis nos et super nivem delabor*

Here, in this quotation from Psalms 1, 7 (Vulgate), Lowell changes
'*me*' to '*nos*' and includes his grandfather (and, presumably, New
England) in his plea for help. And again

> Mother, run to the chalice, and bring back
> Blood on your fingertips for Lazarus who was poor.

In these two passages Lowell employs the full range of his
theology. Two Lazaruses are referred to in the last line: one is the
Lazarus of *Luke* xvi, 19f, who is poor and not allowed to intercede
for a rich man in hell; the other is Lazarus of *John* xi, the symbol of
the Resurrection. Thus, neatly, does Lowell juxtapose two literary
references, conveying both the possibility that his own inter-
cession will be useless and that Winslow may be resurrected on
the last day.

I do not find this juxtaposition—though it has logic—entirely
successful. First, it seems to me insufficient to rescue the poem
from the flaw inherent in Lowell's method of pronouncing judge-

ment. Secondly, there is little poetic quality supporting the Biblical references—'scorched, blue thunderbreasts' is merely vulgar—and, thirdly, the juxtaposition is a mere setting out of literary references: the poetic ambiguity belongs essentially to the Bible, not to Lowell. (The same juxtaposition is made with much greater effect, because a pattern of sound and meaning is built around it, in Eliot's 'Prufrock'.)

I have spent a great deal of time on 'Arthur Winslow' both because it has been so highly praised and because it reveals Lowell's preoccupations so tellingly. For these reasons, since it seemed desirable to discuss one poem at length, 'Arthur Winslow' seemed the best candidate. I find it very seriously flawed, though the quality of the first stanza is remarkable and the final argument has its merits. The main point about the poem, however, is that it is very characteristic, though the rhetoric at the end is more sustained and intelligent than usual. There is a more typical passage concluding 'New Year's Day', where the effect of what Mr. Hamilton calls the 'rhetoric of desperation' is intensified by a highly alliterative iambic line and heavy rhyming, while the sense escapes understanding, though a desperate effort is clearly being made to reach truth:

> Under St. Peter's Bell the parish sea
> . . .
> Swells with its smelt into the burlap shack
> Where Joseph plucks his hand-lines like a harp,
> And hears the fearful *Puer natus est*
> Of Circumcision, and relives the wrack
> And howls of Jesus whom he holds. How sharp
> The burdens of the Law before the beast:
> Time and the grindstone and the knife of God.
> The child is born in blood, O child of blood.

It is impossible to examine each poem in the volume under discussion in detail. But, having argued that, at a central point, 'Arthur Winslow' is a failure, I want to turn to three poems I regard as almost completely successful. If form (in the sense of his use of the juxtaposition) failed Lowell in 'Arthur Winslow', it served him well in these three. They are 'The Holy Innocents', 'Colloquy in Black Rock' and 'Mr. Edwards and the Spider'. I shall take the last poem first, because, technically speaking, the development of the analogy in it, in a grave and measured way, has comparisons with the development of the themes in 'Arthur Winslow'.

'Mr. Edwards and the Spider' is based almost entirely on words taken from the writings of Jonathan Edwards, the eighteenth-century Puritan preacher and amateur entomologist. Using the words of Edwards, adapting his language and imitating his thoughts and ideas, gives Lowell's own poem a subtle strength. Briefly, the analogy in use is that between the death of a spider and the death of a man. The two basic points in the logic of the poem are, firstly, that, considering the power and majesty of God, man can hardly consider himself more significant in His eyes than is a spider to man and secondly, that the essential difference between the spider and man is that man knows death when he sees it—he knows its significance. Behind these two ideas lies the great moral danger delineated in the poem, that man may fall into despair and hell through fancying himself akin in nature to the spider, and thereby not realising the suffering and the punishment to which his nature is prone.

The first stanza is a statement on the nature of the spider, introduced with a delicate portrait of its rural environment. 'They', Edwards says of spiders

> purpose nothing but their ease and die
> Urgently beating east to sunrise and the sea;

The second stanza illustrates the nature of man against this background. There is a treason (against God) in his blood and no works of man can eradicate it. The first flush of enthusiasm, it is said, may serve to resist sin, but man's indolent nature gradually brings him to drop his defences. It is important to note here the significance of the first line: not only does it note simply the impossible gulf of majesty between God and man; it also introduces a suggestion, taken up at the beginning of the last stanza, that the nature of the relationship between man and God is something man cannot understand. It is the majesty of God that calls forth worship and repentance; it is this mystery that leaves an area of hope.

This second stanza reads:

> What are we in the hands of the great God?
> It was in vain you set up thorn and briar
>   In battle array against the fire
>   And treason crackling in your blood;
>   For the wild thorns grow tame
>   And will do nothing to oppose the flame;
>   Your lacerations tell the losing game
>   You play against a sickness past your cure.
> How will the hands be strong? How will the heart endure?

Thus the practice of man is modulated into the practice of the spider, but into the experience of man is injected a series of fiery images of dissolution by fire. In the third, and most difficult stanza, the fire images are carried back to the spider. In the first two and a half lines the David vs. Goliath instinct of man is adverted to (with the spider reference carrying a warning of its invalidity)

> A very little thing, a little worm,
> Or hourglass-blazoned spider, it is said,
> Can kill a tiger.

only to be crushed

> Will the dead
> Hold up his mirror and affirm
> To the four winds the smell
> And flash of his authority?

Dead men tell no tales; certainly they cannot assert the validity of the now dismissed proposition. But to entertain that proposition is to insult the majesty of God and so

> It's well
> If God who holds you to the pit of hell,
> Much as one holds a spider, will destroy,
> Baffle and dissipate your soul.

The stanza goes on to illustrate this judgement by relating how Edwards, as a boy, witnessed the death of a spider in fire. A twist is given to the comparison between man and spider

> There's no long struggle, no desire
> To get up on its feet and fly—
>   It stretches out its feet
> And dies. This is the sinner's last retreat;

In other words, as the next three lines make clear, it is the sinner who meets death with the resignation of the spider.

Now, the second questioning note is introduced

> But who can plumb the sinking of that soul?

In other words, there is a mystery in the relationship between God and man. Edwards, however, invites one of his congregation to consider the one certain fact—of death—and describes a similar method to that of the burning spider. The stanza ends with the superb affirmation of the other certainty, that, because he knows God by his nature, man also knows death: that is the essence and uniqueness of his condition:

> How long would it seem burning! Let there pass
> A minute, ten, ten trillion; but the blaze
> Is infinite, eternal: this is death,
> To die and know it. This is the Black Widow, death.

There is a further possible dimension to the poem. Mr. Staples claims to detect in it some irony (which he does not specify) at the expense of Edwards. The irony may be supposed to be conveyed in two features of the poem: firstly, the doctrine is a stark one, and likely to be unpalatable to Lowell's reader. Second, and perhaps for this reason, the device of indirect speech (through Edwards) which establishes a distance between the poet and the speaker, may be taken as Lowell's way of objectifying and distancing Edwards. This may be taken to be ironic, with the irony conveyed in the method, though not in the lines; the point could be sustained by the fact that almost all the words are Edwards's words. But the last line is indisputably Lowell: they are his words, this is his voice. Supposing the structure of irony to exist in the rest of the poem (and I cannot wholly persuade myself that it does), the last line unequivocally encompasses and transcends that structure. It is as though, speaking with two voices throughout, Lowell suddenly speaks with a single, powerful voice that transcends Edwards and the reader's response alike: the truth is as Edwards saw it, even if, seeing it *he* did not wholly comprehend it. This reading, with the master control in the last line, would make the poem even better than I have supposed it to be. It is with regret that I find the point uncertain.

Nonetheless, this seems to me to be one of the most nearly perfect poems Lowell has written. Though the doctrine here may seem superficially similar to the one whose expression I severely criticised in 'The Quaker Graveyard' (p. 17) and 'The First Sunday in Lent' (p. 16) its form in this poem is entirely different.

First, the doctrine, though simple, is entirely coherent. I will state it again for clarity. The gulf between the majesty of God and the insignificance of man is too great to be understood, or, in any significant way, acted upon. It can, however, be illustrated, by comparing man to a spider. This illustration, however, conceals as much as it reveals. For the nature of man and the nature of the spider are quite different, particularly in the way in which they understand death. Knowing death is what distinguishes man's nature. He can grasp the term of that experience even in life and, by doing so, can gain a hint of his relationship to God. That hint— and here is the real and unvarnished content of Lowell's theology —is an imitation of the most profound, and only knowable, reality. Once it is appreciated, no earthly experience can compare to it.

The doctrine is less narrow than it appears, and, illustrated as it is here, with the images hammered into gold from Edwards's own prose, and the whole integrated into the flexible yet subtly strong metre of Donne's 'Nocturnal upon St. Lucy's Day', one of the finest poetic instruments available for sustaining and containing an argument, its narrowness is concealed. The point of the identification with the spider is so true, and each separate argument is so felicitously placed, that the whole structure establishes its own authority.

Nonetheless, the doctrine is narrow and that is a weakness, not so much, perhaps, of this poem as of other poetry in the same vein. First, if only one experience is truly valid or worthwhile, then the capacity for explaining or illustrating it is severely limited. All, indeed, is contained in the last two lines of this poem. Secondly, by this doctrine and its implications the validity of the practice of poetry itself must be called into question. Thirdly, the knowledge the poem depicts is not humanly enriching: useful action is denied to man, who must, it appears, simply contemplate death strenuously and do nothing else. Given, then, the quality of the achievement here, and bearing in mind the support Lowell made for himself from Edwards and Donne, it is clear that there is little that is self-sustaining in this poem. Like the other good poems in the volume, it stands on its own for quality.

My second poem is 'The Holy Innocents', also a religious poem and also one ending in an annunciatory discovery. The basic framework of the poem is that of a simple anecdote: it describes a team of oxen pulling a cart up a hill. Within that framework— and using a metrical and rhyme scheme that shifts gradually and connectedly between the three phases contained in two stanzas— Lowell sets down a complex scheme of analogies. At the end of the second stanza these analogies take the form of juxtapositions, with the logical apparatus pared away to give greater intensity, as with Wordsworth. Initially, the final analogies are shocking and their logical connections not, perhaps, instantly apparent. However, as these logical connections become apparent, the impact of the poem is increased: the sound pattern is very, and the rhyme pattern quite, complex, while the logic of the analogies is simple and traditional (though in each case given a special turn), with one exception. This contrast has the effect of enriching quite conventional metaphors with meaning. Because, moreover, the metaphors themselves relate to the mystery of God's relations with man, their structure bears enrichment. Finally the process of enriching the metaphors—and the whole relationship between them and the analogies—sets the relationship of man and history to God in a series of poetic images.

The outer analogy—the one enclosing, as it were, the others within its circle—is between the team of oxen struggling up the hill and the year 1945 struggling up the hill of history. This analogy is achieved, however, not by a logical or even para-logical argument, but by a sudden leap of the imagination, following closely on carefully prepared and, once, a difficult Biblical, analogy. From the establishment of the main analogy in the second stanza, however, the poem rushes swiftly to its conclusion, a swiftness made all the more remarkable by the understated drama of the final analogy.

The poem opens quietly and conventionally with a description of the physical scene:

> Listen, the hay-bells tinkle as the cart
> Wavers on rubber tires along the tar
> And cindered ice below the burlap mill
> And ale-wife run. The oxen drool and start
> In wonder at the fenders of a car,
> And blunder hugely up St. Peter's hill.

'St. Peter's' is the first possibly religious emphasis after the title. In these six lines, however, Lowell, while setting an ordinary, though very precisely and (in a minor key) imaginatively des-cribed scene, introduces certain elements of the unfamiliar and strange into his scene—ice, wonder, drool (though physically true it is out of key with the clear simplicity of earlier words) and 'blunder hugely'. These prepare the way for the first analogy, the one most difficult to establish. The slow pace of the first six lines is quickly altered, the end rhymes change and, in the next line, the pause or cesura shifts to between the last and second last words of the line. Within the general framework, then, the pattern, style and purpose of the poem suddenly change:

These are the undefiled by woman—their

I pause here so that the reader can see the whole analogy and (with 'their') the beginnings of the way in which the poet proposes to illustrate it. The meaning of the analogy is expressed in its source in *Revelation*, xiv, 3–4.

'These are they which were not defiled with women; for they are virgin. These are they who follow the Lamb whithersoever he goeth.'

The analogy as expressed in the line is worth delaying over. Once it is established, its meanings become clear, and Lowell, as we shall see, rushes on to the end of the stanza without giving the reader time for second thoughts.

The establishment of the analogy is the difficult point. I cannot explain altogether completely why it is I find it satisfactory. I think it is, firstly, that the shift of mood, meaning and technique is so sudden that one starts and, secondly, that when one looks at the line again and sees its source, implications of its meanings are suddenly available to one. Then, as one's eye goes back over the earlier lines of the stanza, further implications become apparent.

The equation in the analogy is between the simple brutes of burden and the simple followers of Christ. It is enriched by reference back. The oxen are 'undefiled by women', that is, unusual and out of place—at odds—with secular life at any time. The fourth and fifth lines give that alienation an especially modern turn. Thus the proposition is established that the followers of Christ are alienated from the world of man and, in a special way, from the world of twentieth-century man.

The rush to the end of the first stanza establishes Lowell historically in the time of Jesus: the poem has moved to a new level. I shall repeat all of the last four lines:

These are the undefiled by women—their
Sorrow is not the sorrow of this world:
King Herod shrieking vengeance at the curled
Up knees of Jesus choking in the air,

With the first of these lines Lowell establishes his new level. The run over to the second line brings him further into this new world and illustrates an important theme from it—the superiority of sensibility it enjoys over the material world. The last pair of lines illustrate the kind of activity of the material world which can distress, but can have no real effect on those suffering a more elevated sorrow. Not only has Lowell created a new world with his analogy, he has rapidly delineated its character as well.

But the analogy itself is not lost sight of. The comma at its end shows the last line of the first stanza as a run over to the second. In that last line Jesus is deeply identified with his followers, for it is at him that Herod shrieks vengeance. That identification is advanced a stage in the first line of the second stanza

A king of speechless clods and infants.

In the first stanza the relationship between the followers and Jesus has two features: the movement takes place from them to him; he is identified with them only in so far as they suffer for him and he suffers the same attacks as they do. Secondly, the relationship is entirely a traditionally Christian one in that it emphasises the common alienation of Christ's followers from the world about them.

To this is added, in this first line of the second stanza, another traditional description of Jesus, one beloved of the Bible and supposedly used contemptuously by His enemies, as a king of mere children: the description is given point by 'clods and infants', 'clods' standing for the oxen and 'infants', in the light of the later Christmas reference, identifying the Saviour with the infants massacred in his place.

In the following lines the hint (in 'fenders of a car') in the first stanza of a peculiarly modern alienation is developed; the pace of the lines suddenly alters from the high pitch that ran over between the stanza to a revival of the activity of the labouring oxen. We are switched back to an earlier established mood and place and the second analogy is made:

>   Still
> The world out-Herods Herod; and the year,
> The nineteen-hundred forty-fifth of grace,
> Lumbers with losses up the clinkered hill
> Of our purgation!

This is a passage that I pause over again and again, in admiration of his various moods, its perfect control, the weight each word and phrase carries and the technical perfection of the whole. Note, in the third line, the use of an American idiom to give the very date the same pattern of sense and sound as the climb of the oxen, note the irony in 'grace' and the controlled under-statement of 'with losses' of the last year of the World War, with 'purgation' in the following line expanding that theme and deepening its resonance. Note, above all, that the analogy here is between the cart and the world of time: that world is the burden the followers of Christ bear, as the oxen pull the cart. The sheer grace and control of every touch in these lines is what sustains the point of the analogy and bears it over the gulf of reason.

Now, yet again, Lowell returns to the beginning of his poem. The journey of the oxen had a point: the return to that point is one of the most beautiful effects of the poem

>   and the oxen near
> The worn foundations of their resting-place,
> The holy manger where their bed is corn
> And holly torn for Christmas.

Now the third analogy, surrounded by a pause for inspection and juxtaposed

>   If they die,
> As Jesus, in the harness, who will mourn?

With 'in the harness' the complex and interlocking series of relationships, built up through transition from analogy to analogy, to juxtaposition, finds a still centre. Whereas Lowell has up to now reminded us that the oxen are the followers of Jesus, has mediated for the followers through the oxen to Jesus and (in the last line of the first and the first line of the second, stanza) mediated back again, partly through the same image, suddenly he establishes a direct relationship between the oxen and Jesus. That relationship has its own terrible resonance, for Jesus's death 'in the harness' can only refer to the reality of the crucifixion. Again, each reference, each juxtaposition, carries its own enrichment and enriches the whole.

Still Lowell is not finished, though he has only one line to go. If he had stopped at 'mourn?' he would have written a fine poem, of rare beauty. It would have rested on the convention of alienation of God and his followers from society, conveyed, generally, in all the images of silence, speechlessness and inability to communicate. But there is a more terrible alienation, that of the majesty of God:

Lamb of the shepherds, Child, how still you lie.

The follower of Jesus, labouring up the hill of life with his burden, may be tempted to console himself through his identification with Christ. As there is silence between the follower and the world, so there is silence between Jesus and the world, not only through the world's hostility but through the identification of Christ with his followers—alien, speechless and children. That identification is furthered by the fact that Christ is a Child; he is also a lamb, hence the potential consolation. But there is also a silence between Christ and his followers. Christ lies still: there may be neither reward nor consolation at the end of the journey (the question mark suggests a doubt). We are back with Edwards and the spider.

Dr. Dermot Fenlon, however, suggests to me that I have misunderstood this last line. In his reading it is an affirmation, an expression of awe in the presence of the child, a delineation of the

3*

wonder with which the Christian regards his Saviour. Dr. Fenlon makes the analogy with 'Lord, Lord why hast thou forsaken us?', which he interprets as affirmative rather than despairing. Should this be unequivocally established, the affirmation rescued from circumstance in the last line would make the poem greater than I have suggested. It is not, I believe however, an interpretation that does arise out of the circumstances of the poem itself, out of its texture. Dr. Fenlon, however, suggests that his and my interpretations are congruent with each other, that there is an ambiguity in the poem and that, in a matter of this moment, this ambiguity diminishes the achievement. The point seems to me to be disputable. Dr. Fenlon's interpretation does not appear to me to take account sufficiently of the emphasis on 'still' in the last line: that emphasis seems to me to be one of terror, bleak and unvarnished, and more effective as such than any conceivable, more obvious alternative. The stillness of death, moreover, follows on the death in the previous two lines and can arise out of it. In conscience, however, I cannot say that I am absolutely certain. My doctrinal point is coherent with the way I understood Lowell's doctrine as expressed elsewhere and particularly in 'Mr. Edwards and the Spider'; Dr. Fenlon's point is coherent with the ambiguity and evasion that I also find characteristic of Lowell.

There is no fault in this poem as a poem. But, as with 'Mr. Edwards and the Spider', there is a serious danger—a flaw—in the doctrine behind it. That doctrine, it should be said, is not Catholic but Calvinist: in his religious phase Lowell's inspiration was rarely Catholic, except in some images and doctrinal references. A central role in Catholic theology, for example, is played by the Virgin Mary. To her role Lowell pays obeisance. Yet, in the two occasions cited where Mary appears—'The Quaker Graveyard' and 'Arthur Winslow'—his usage is deficient where it is not vulgar: he can carry no majesty through Her. He cannot use a religious idea not in his bones. The well-spring of his drive—the vision of God he saw—was in the theology of his ancestors. These poems are concerned with the annunciation of God to man: they are didactic and public poems. But their foundation is narrow; they draw little if at all on the quotidian experience of men; they

illustrate the meaning of a doctrine rather than explore meaning
and effects; they induce awe rather than understanding; and few
men—certainly not Lowell the poet—could bear to contemplate
for long the unsparing vision presented in the poetry, or find
means and resources wherewith to illustrate it as a life's work. In
his fundamental identification with this doctrine Lowell suffers;
although there can be no gainsaying the achievement of these
poems, it is in that very achievement that Lowell is most clearly
the victim of Maule's curse.

Unlike 'Arthur Winslow' these two poems describe little if at
all the secular world they condemn. That task can be avoided
because the brilliant exploration of authoritative themes, allied to
the basically and fundamentally authoritative nature of the primal
propositions of the poems, constitute sufficient resources in themselves. Nonetheless, the infrequent irruption of the contemporary
world—towards which Lowell is continually concerned to point
his shaft—should be noted. That is the world that Lowell must
reach: it is the world he can least successfully handle in its
multifarious detail with authority.

I do not propose to examine 'Colloquy in Black Rock' at the
same length. A very good account of it is given by Mr. Staples
and, though I do not feel he has fully pursued the ramifications of
the poem, these should be quickly apparent to the attentive reader.
Some of Mr. Staples's comments are, however, worth putting
together: although he illustrates well the great achievement of the
poem, he is even better on its character. I will quote the first
stanza again to give a general illustration of this:

> Here the jack-hammer jabs into the ocean;
> My heart, you race and stagger and demand
> More blood-gangs for your nigger-brass percussions,
> Till I, the stunned machine of your devotion,
> Clanging upon this cymbal of a hand,
> Am rattled screw and footloose.

Mr. Staples illustrates the central movement of the poem very
well:

'The "colloquy" of the title is between the poet and his "heart", a term that is used ambiguously, in every stanza, to refer to both the physical organ and the soul. On the physical level, the acceleration of the heartbeat has the ironic effect of speeding up the biological processes until they become catabolic, and "all discussions end in . . . death." Conversely, however, as the physical heart loses its vitality, the soul benefits from this quickening, as it prepares for the reception of the Holy Spirit.'

As Mr. Staples says, the poem is 'unexpectedly orthodox'; it is 'an anthem celebrating the miracle of the Eucharist . . .' (and therefore specifically Catholic). What gives it its effect is 'the brutal violence of his metaphors'. Death is to be accompanied by the destruction of the physical world, conveyed in a jumble of images of dissolution

> End in low water, slump, and dumps and death.
> My heart, beat faster, faster. In Black Mud
> Hungarian machinists give their blood
> For the martyr Stephen, who was stoned to death.

What contains and controls the centrifugal violence of the image is what Mr. Staples describes as 'a tight, almost symmetrical pattern of sestets and quatrains of iambic pentameter, with the quatrains serving as antiphons.' The form, in other words, controls perceived destruction—giving the poet great freedom in his account of it—and enables Lowell to guide it to its destination.

In the last stages of the journey the essence of the destruction—'mud'—is preserved. 'Mud', indeed, is the most daringly used word in the poem. In turning 'black rod' to 'black mud' Lowell most effectively conveys the destruction he is describing. But in a brilliant inversion of the usual concept of the behaviour of matter, its further dissolution is achieved by the positive, concentrated, integral image of the kingfisher, symbolising God as the Holy Ghost which re-concentrates experience. Thus, in the re-integration of the essence of life—heart as soul—man is brought to God through the destruction of his physical world:

Christ walks on the black water. In Black Mud
Darts the Kingfisher. On Corpus Christi, heart,
Over the drum-beat of St. Stephen's choir
I hear him, *Stupor Mundi*, and the mud
Flies from his hunching wings and beak—my heart,
The blue kingfisher dives on you in fire.

There are other good poems in *Poems 1938-49*—'Falling Asleep over the Aeneid' and 'Mother Marie Therese' as well as 'The First Sunday in Lent' are examples—but nothing else achieves the intensity, complexity or success of the three just examined. Even in dealing with this trio, one can see, not so much differences of achievement as differences of method. In 'Colloquy in Black Rock' it is the metre that contains the violence and dissolution, the centrifugal character, of the images; in the other two poems the intellectual starting point is the analogical conceptions, which are used to enrich each other with such skill.

There is another source of strength, out of which Lowell constructs poetry, in this volume; that is the literary originals which he adapts. Edwards's own prose provides the starting point for 'Mr. Edwards and the Spider' and the source material, being both an inspiration and a starting point, serves to an extent to control the poet's volcanic impulses. The first poem in the volume—'The Exile's Return'—sees a somewhat similar process at work. Here Lowell looks at the tragic effects of the war in Germany, with a characteristic vision of its counter-productive effects:

> The search-guns click and spit and split up timber
> And nick the slate-roofs on the Holstenwall
> Where torn-up tilestones crown the victor.

But, the ruin of the landscape once established, Lowell shifts from this mood to one of hope, tempered with a characteristic shrug of despair:

> When the unseasoned liberators roll
> Into the Market Square, ground arms before
> The Rathaus; but already lily-stands

> Burgeon the risen Rhineland, and a rough
> Cathedral lifts its eye. Pleasant enough,
> *Voi ch'entrate*, and your life is in your hands.

This is quite a good poem. Little verbal felicities may be noted —like the precision of 'ground arms'—but the real substance of the poem comes from a translation of *Tonio Kröger*. There are, of course, degrees in the business of adaptation: but it may be said at once that this is a much less remarkable use of source material by Lowell than is to be found in 'Mr. Edwards and the Spider'. None-theless, the material has had a distinct influence on the poet: it has channelled his energies and disciplined his impulses.

When this sought out discipline is only partially or not at all in action we get the kind of breach of logic seen in 'Arthur Winslow' or the railing of 'New Year's Day'. And, for all the many excellent passages in *Poems 1938–49*, few of the poems are without serious flaws. Some of these flaws are obvious enough— the increase of energy at the expense of point, a pathetic crudity of expression, as in 'scorched blue thunderbreasts' or

> It must have been a Friday. I could hear
> The top-floor typist's thunder and the beer
> That you had brought in cases hurt my head;
> I'd sent the pillows flying from my bed,
>   —*Between the Porch and Altar*

or a bringing of apocalyptic rhetoric to bear on a delicate struc-ture, as in 'The First Sunday in Lent'. In addition, though no one would ever claim that, as a poet, Lowell lacked energy, the energy often runs to seed in a purely local effect. Mr. Holloway, for example, translates a phrase of Virgil as meaning 'its face is wet with big drops' which Lowell poetises as 'stately tears/Lather its teeth'. No doubt, this is, as Mr. Holloway says, an achievement in 'intricate suggestiveness'. But, in a poem ('Falling Asleep over the Aeneid') deficient in its central logical structure, it suggests a rather misdirected effort. Both Mr. Holloway (who refers to the 'Brilliantly intricate and interwoven, brilliantly brocaded and vivid' work of 'Falling Asleep') and Mr. Staples are, in my view, far too inclined to be deceived by Lowell's decorativeness. It seems to induce a certain awe. Mr. Staples, for example, is continuously found referring to Lowell's scholarship ('the breadth of his scholarship' is a typical phrase) when—let us be blunt about this—Lowell is no more a scholar than Yeats was: they are both reasonably well read men looking out material for poetry. To find a great poet who was also a scholar, and whose poetry is 'scholarly' in the sense that Mr. Staples speaks of Lowell's work, we must go back to Johnson; even then we do find the shade of a real classical critic—Dr. Parr—who yielded to no one in his admiration for Johnson, demurring.

I make these points, not to deride Mr. Staples and Mr. Holloway, who have contributed greatly to our understanding of Lowell, but to suggest that there is built in to our appreciation of *Poems 1938–49* a kind of judgement that misses both the essential achievement and the essential failure of these poems. Seeing all periods of history as the same, Lowell, in the first phase of his career, tried to achieve an exact description of man's direct relationship to God: the rest is enrichment of the relevance of that relationship to all human thought and argument.

It is not a lack of talent, of taste or of energy that leads Lowell into the failures of *Poems 1938–49*. The failures are a result of the inapplicability of his didactic doctrine about man's relationship to God. Or, if you like, a failure on his part to expand that doctrine, to give it meaning for the life of man in the world: the relationship between talent and doctrine is normally as well as psychologically obscure. I have suggested that the world of man and the world of the spirit and of perception are divided from one another in Lowell's poems. I want to suggest also that the insight —the contemporaneity of all history—which is dependent on, indeed, a consequence of, the doctrine, tends to corrupt the poetry.

In 'Concord' Lowell describes a town in which, now, 'Ten thousand Fords are idle here in search of a tradition'; he describes the history of the town in the context of New England history; he contrasts its Christian faith to its worship of 'Mammon's

unbridled industry' and finally refers (a recurrent theme) to the
wars of his ancestors against the Indians

> The death-dance of King Philip and his scream
> Whose echo girdled this imperfect globe.

The local effects here are often good; there is a nice irony in
'Ten thousand Fords' and a totally unexpected and telling use of
'transfix' in a couplet where prosaic logic might expect 'embrace'
or 'encompass'. Of a crucifix

> How can your whited spindling arms transfix
> Mammon's unbridled industry,

But, partly because of, not merely the success, but the strange-
ness, the local effects, the last two lines are crucial, and the last line
is a disaster, a disaster of the doctrine and the insight that dominate
his best work. One can see the pastoral implications of 'imperfect'
but none of the numerous logical justification of its use can com-
pensate for the way it shatters, not only the argument, but the
fine, free run of the previous line; and with another flaccid word—
'globe'—in a poem of strong words, the effect becomes, not weak
only, but tawdry and puling.

And yet one can see what Lowell is trying to get at: he is trying
to universalise his judgement and his insight, as the intended
dimensions of the last line show. The attempt fails because, in the
conditions of this poem, the local phases—unlike the interlocking
phases of the three great poems—neither support nor justify each
other. There is no development in this poem, whether of
chronology or argument. It is a scattering of condemnations. No
structure gives drive to the conclusion and the conclusion is, in
consequence, highly personal and weak.

In 'Salem' Lowell descends to a jeer. What is at most merely a
description of seamen at work suddenly becomes a rather pom-
pous judgement, not only on Salem now, but on Salem in the
past, with no reason or justification advanced in the poem:

Where was it that New England bred the men
Who quartered the Leviathan's fat flanks
And fought the British Lion to his knees?

Examples could be multiplied. They are all examples of a failure in the grain of the poetry, a failure that is, not only as seen by our objective judgement of the result, but a failure in what Lowell set out to do and in what he clearly strives to achieve. It would be tedious to go through all of the poems in this volume sorting out the different ways in which corruption takes effect. I want, therefore, to quote one poem, 'Children of Light', which is the most abstract encapsulation of Lowell's historical view of New England and then to suggest one more general feature of his work which prepares the way for the new development in *Life Studies*, before examining the ultimate failure of the early work in 'Thanksgiving's Over'. I would add, however, that some of the adaptations and imitations in this volume will re-appear in the chapter on *Imitations* and that the relationship between achievement and failure will be more closely scrutinised in my chapter on 'The Quaker Graveyard' and 'The Mills of the Kavanaughs'.

'Children of Light' reads:

Our fathers wrung their bread from stocks and stones
And fenced their gardens with the Redman's bones;
Embarking from the Nether Land of Holland,
Pilgrims unhouseled by Geneva's night,
They planted here the Serpent's seeds of light;
And here the pivoting searchlights probe to shock
The riotous glasshouses built on rock,
And candles gutter by an empty altar,
And light is where the landless blood of Cain
Is burning, burning the unburied grain.

This short poem of despair is not entirely unsuccessful; the image in the second line is sharp and effective and the irony in the third, though cumbersome, may be judged to come across. But, as the poem proceeds, the references and the intended scope of the argument become less precise and less related, less specific and

therefore less powerful. It is clear from the line 'Pilgrims unhouseled by Geneva's night' that Lowell is taking his condemnation of the sinfulness of his New England forebears back beyond
America itself, back to the Calvinistic doctrines the original
settlers brought from Europe.

It is, one suspects, lines like the fourth and fifth of this poem

> Pilgrims unhouseled by Geneva's night,
> They planted here the Serpent's seeds of light;

that have so often led critics to suppose that Lowell, in his attack
on the corruption of New England history, is attacking also the
Predestinarian theology that sustained its religious vision. The
truth is that Lowell himself seems to have been ambiguous and
uncertain on that point. The condemnation of the spirit of
Calvinism in 'Children of Light' is quite unequivocal but, as we
have seen, both the content and the style of Lowell's own most
powerful judgements are Calvinistic rather than Catholic. It seems
that Lowell was in a position in which Catholic beliefs and Predestinarian impulses were at war within him. On the whole, he
was quite clear about his intention to condemn the secular past of
New England, and quite controlled enough and certain in his
condemnation—as in 'The Quaker Graveyard', 'Arthur Winslow' and 'Salem'—to make wry, or ironic and partly successful
references either to the nobler impulses of his human subjects or
to the more elevated regard New Englanders had for their own
achievement in history.

The difficulties from which his failures arose are to be found
both in his failure to transmit his historical judgement through the
present to the past (as in 'Arthur Winslow' Part III) and in his
failure to find the true origin in men of the evil impulse which
roused his anger: the first of these points depends to a degree on
the second and his uncertainty about the second leads to specific
uncertainty about the basic nature and effect of the central Puritan
impulse of the unredeemability of man.

That there is something of deeply evil tendency in man is never
questioned in *Poems 1938-49*. But since this impulse is almost

always seen through the relatively specific past and present of New England it is difficult to establish where Lowell drew the line between evil in human nature and evil as manifested in the history of his own province. A remarkable passage in a difficult poem, 'As a Plane Tree by the Water' (in which Lowell speaks of this 'planned/Babel of Boston where our money talks/And multiplies the darkness of a land') throws light on both the rhetorical certainty of his condemnation and the inner uncertainty of his judgement:

> The flies, the flies, the flies of Babylon
> Buzz in my ear-drums while the devil's long
> Dirge of the people detonates the hour
> For floating cities where his golden tongue
> Enchants the masons of the Babel Tower
> To raise tomorrow's city to the sun
> That never sets upon these hell-fire streets
> Of Boston, where the sunlight is a sword
> Striking at the witholder of the Lord:
> Flies, flies are on the plane tree, on the streets.

This is an entirely visionary and emotional poem, and, as such, rather good. For their effect, such poems depend on attracting the senses while lulling the reason: sound and movement of the lines are, therefore, highly important. There is a clean, flowing, confident movement in the passage quoted; with our knowledge of the rest of his work we can see what Lowell is driving at and, between the first and last lines the images enjoy a specificity more apparent than real. This is the technique of pseudo-reference: there is, in the poem, fairly explicit reference to a non-existent symbolic value, that is, the evidence entitling the poet to make his judgement is either concealed or non-existent but the characteristics outlined above create the illusion that this evidence is presented. Thus we have a pleasing configuration of sound, but no concreteness of meaning.

A justification for this mode appears in the third stanza when

> Flies strike the miraculous waters of the iced
> Atlantic and the eyes of Bernadette
> Who saw Our Lady standing in the cave
> At Massabielle, saw her so squarely that
> Her vision put out reason's eyes.

What this means is that Bernadette's ordinary human capacity for seeing reality was surpassed by her vision (the word is double-meaning, standing both for ordinary sight and for superior, spiritual appearances and insight) of Mary that she saw. The condition of Boston is so offensive that it ('Flies strike' . . . 'the eyes of Bernadette') assails the quality of this superior vision. The comparison, however, is also implied between Bernadette's capacity to see and Lowell's capacity to see—in his case the degradation of Boston.

It is a complete and subtle argument which endeavours to excuse the stanza first quoted. It is also (by the use of 'Flies' to attack Bernadette) the only justification offered for the meaning of the refrain appearing in the last line of each stanza

> 'Flies, flies are on the plane tree, on the streets'

in which refrain we have the real judgement of the poem. Yet it adds no real weight to, or explanation of the meaning of either refrain or judgement, the conviction of which are not significantly increased beyond the sound pattern they enjoy and the vague connotation of the words. Pseudo-reference, then, dominates; and that is almost invariably the technique employed by a poet uncertain of his resources for judgement and evading the consequences of that uncertainty. Uncertainty is at the root of Lowell's violence: we would do well not to forget how often it produces evasion as well.

Now it may be objected that, in the case of the three poems I selected for high praise, some of the same kinds of faults are present and, in particular, that, in 'Colloquy in Black Rock', Lowell allows himself indulgence in the vice of imitative form, that is, wanting to convey disintegration he disintegrated the logic and rationality of his structure.

These objections would not be without force but, in so far as
they might be arguments against the method of criticism I am
employing, they would represent a failure to perceive and discriminate. In 'Mr. Edwards and the Spider' the delicate structure
of the poem rests on a convention—the existence of God—which
is entirely acceptable as such. Once the existence of God is accepted
(as a convention, it does not need to be established) the deductions
—as of the comparison between spider and man—are entirely
rational: both the rational and the poetic logic of the piece are
thereafter irrefutable. In 'The Holy Innocents' Lowell uses a
narrative framework within which he carefully and patiently
develops a series of analogies the weight and justification of which
are increased and enriched retrospectively as the poem develops.
With the single exception of the first ('undefiled by woman')
analogy all rest on evidence presented in the poem and I
have given my reasons for accepting the presentation of that
analogy.

In 'Colloquy in Black Rock', however, the case is altered. Here
what sustains the logical meaning of the disintegrating images is
the development throughout of certain poetic meanings and
usages, notably of 'rock' as compared to 'mud' and of 'heart' and
'soul'. On the other hand, it would be wrong to deny that there is
an element of imitative form in the poem: it simply seems to me
that its merits greatly outweigh this fault.

Nonetheless, the presence of imitative form is a weakness, as the
narrowness of the doctrine in 'Mr. Edwards and the Spider' and
even in 'The Holy Innocents' is a weakness, not so much for those
poems as for Lowell's poetry as a whole: my point is that his
characteristic faults can be deduced from his best poetry. In the
best work, and particularly in 'Colloquy', one can see faults and
corrupting tendencies brought under control by the poet. 'The
spiritual control in a poem . . .' as Winters says 'is simply a manifestation of spiritual control within the poet.'[2] No doubt this is
always, and was always, true, though this statement by Winters
conceals a difficulty, the one I have claimed to detect by suggesting that the entry of the poet personally into the poem (in public
poetry in particular) was a significant moment in the history of

English literature, the implications of which are fully present in Lowell's poetry.

I do not believe that any sensitive person could read through *Poems 1938–49* without being struck on every hand by the personal presence of Lowell and the unique character of his personal voice. I have tried to indicate in these two chapters my conviction that, in actuality, that personal voice and character constitute the ultimate driving force—authority, if you like—of the poems and that Lowell's tensions and difficulties arose from the clash between personality and intention, the intention or ambition to write public poetry. The availability of other resources to Lowell was limited, as his doctrines were narrow. Consequently, the development of form absorbed most of his energies. But there *were* other resources, the imagery of the Catholic Church, the doctrine of Puritanism and a view of history among them. When the poetry is good or even great all these elements come into harmonious relation with each other: it is then still possible to detect potential corruption in the resources and hence—since resources are not really corrupt; only the use of them is—deduce lack of harmony and control in the personality. In cases of success faults in the form are rarely detectable.

The various sub-devices and characteristics of the poetry I have often noted as faults or abuses or weaknesses of one kind or another—analogy, juxtaposition, transition, pseudo-reference, imitative form—are screens or protective earth words thrown up to cover gaps in the relationship between the poet and his materials. The amazing contrast between height and depth in this first phase of Lowell's work I ascribe to his failure ever to establish a stable or continuously harmonious relationship between personality, forms, resources, doctrine, and insights. In a perfect critical world that would be taken simply as a measure of his failure (or, on the other side of the coin, limited achievement) as a poet. In fact I would like to take into account as well the historical background sketched in the first chapter, which I take to have imposed heavy burdens on him. I should add that I do not put forward this view in any way as an excuse: it is simply an expression of my belief that, by understanding our difficulties and limitations, we may overcome them or reverse their effects.

The poems in *The Mills of the Kavanaughs*, and particularly 'Thanksgiving's Over', represent the disintegration of this precariously balanced system. Most of them are, in varying degrees, unintelligible (Lowell later referred, in the Note to *For the Union Dead*, to one of them, 'David and Bathsheba in the public garden' as 'confusing' and replaced it with a clarified version: I shall examine the two versions together in Chapter Five and demonstrate a growing hostility to the Christianity which was a bedrock of the early work.

'Thanksgiving's Over' recounts the dream of the husband of a German-American Catholic who jumped from a window and later died in a sanatorium. Most of the lines are the wife's: she believes she is the Virgin Mary, that her toy parrot is the Holy Ghost and that her husband is attempting sacrilegiously to break their relationship. She tried to escape through suicide or to punish him through homicide. The hallucination is, of course, really the husband's (that is, Lowell's), since the dream is his and its manic phases are interrupted by cries for help from his wife and doubts about the rightness of his own actions and impulses.

A detailed analysis of this poem would serve little purpose, though there is a passage of extraordinary clarity and significance which I will quote later. Two general points are worth noting. First, the most significant fault of the poem is the extreme corruption of imitative form: madness is described by madness in the argument of the poem:

> Blue cloud! There, ruin toils not, though infirm:
> Our water-shed! Our golden weathercocks
> Are creaking: Fall is here, and starlings. Flocks
> Scavenge for El Dorado in the hemlocks.
> O Michael, hurry up and ring my bell.
> Ring, ring for me! . . . Why do you make us kneel?
> Why are we praying?

Secondly, the poem is not beyond analysis and this fact is

represented in its intricate formal structure: the rhyme scheme and metrical pattern are given by Mr. Staples as follows:

Stanza 1   a a b b c d d c c e e e e f f g g e h h h
             (5 5 5 5 5 5 5 5 5 5 5 5 5 5 5 5 5 5 5 5)

2   a b c a a c c b d d b e f a g h h d a b i b h j j
     (5 5 5 5 4 5 2 5 5 2 4 5 5 5 5 3 5 5 3 5 5 6 5 5 5)

3   a b c a a c c b d d b e f a g h h d a b i b h j j j
     (5 5 5 5 4 5 2 5 5 2 4 5 5 5 5 3 5 5 3 5 5 6 5 5 5 5)

4   a b c c b b a d d a e f c g e e d c a h a i j j
     (5 5 5 4 5 2 5 5 2 4 5 5 5 3 5 5 3 6 5 5 5 5 5 5)

5   a b c a a c c b d d b e f a g h h d a b i b h j j
     (5 5 5 5 4 5 2 4 4 2 4 5 5 5 5 3 5 5 3 5 5 6 5 5 5)

6   a b b a c c d a e e d f a g f g
     (5 5 5 5 5 5 5 5 5 5 5 5 5 5 5 5)

The technical movement of the poem can be described: it makes a moderately coherent pattern. The argument can be described, but it is the manic recounting of manic experience: the dream convention, which should be the controlling element, is inextricably confused with the madness. Nonetheless there is the passage of clarity I mentioned:

> Now Michael sleeps,
> Thanksgiving's over, nothing is for keeps:
> New earth, new sky, new life: I hear the word
> Of Brother Francis, child and bird, descend,
> Calling the war of Michael a pretend;
> The Lord is Brother Parrot, and a friend.

The description of God as a parrot is madness. In that madness lies a truth: God is no different from man and beast; that is, He does not exist; Michael's (Lowell's) war—all the struggle of life and poetry so far—had no meaning. With this renunciation, the first phase of Lowell's career ends.

3 'The Quaker Graveyard' and 'The Mills of the Kavanaughs'

'THE QUAKER GRAVEYARD in Nantucket' and 'The Mills of the Kavanaughs' are Lowell's most sustained efforts at (judged by contemporary standards) long poems. The first is an elegy for his cousin Warren Winslow, lost at sea during the Second World War. The second is an account of the disintegration of a family—the Kavanaughs: in the first version, published in *The Kenyon Review* in the winter of 1951, Catholic doctrine and imagery were entangled with classical myth and visions of hellfire; in the revised version, published in the volume of the same title, the positive Catholic symbolism had disappeared; the poem therefore represents an important stage of Lowell's farewell to Catholicism, and of his search for an alternative system or systems.

I will have occasion to discuss later (in Chapter Six) the importance to Lowell's work of his study of other poets and their methods, made practical rather than academic by his imitations. I have mentioned already my belief that the process of imitation, whether by the adaptation of other poems or their technical structures, or by the adaptation of prose, often lends sinew both to Lowell's argument and poetic. That is true of 'The Quaker Graveyard' where the Italian *canzone* is adapted in a manner similar to that of Milton in *Lycidas* (though one suspects that the model is Milton rather than the original Italian). In my view, the pentameter structure of the stanzas (which is flexible, the rhymes being repeated only twice), as well as such of the characteristics of the traditional elegy as he has retained, has given Lowell, in this poem, a strong formal structure which helps considerably the consecutive carrying forward of his argument. At the same time, this is only a help: the real success of the poem lies in Lowell's ability to develop and extend the doctrine of his first three volumes sufficiently to sustain him over a long course. The long form, in its closer structure, assists: it is also a challenge.

As between the Puritan theology outlines in its basic form and implications in the last chapter, and the more flexible but (for poetry) equally ultimately destructive Catholic mysticism which overlays Lowell's earlier career, 'The Quaker Graveyard' inclines towards the latter. In the last chapter I defined the Puritan theology that governed Lowell so strongly. It, of course, had in real life a solvent, in that it was a creed that had to be come to terms with in day to day life. Spread through man's secular life, it could be ennobling or restrictive; it certainly severely marked, for good and ill, the civilisation that grew up with it in America. Logically, it was a creed that could not be lived with, but men had to live. In poetry, however, the doctrine had other effects, one advantage and one major and ultimate disadvantage.

Ultimately, poetry is the most concentrated form of human utterance: 'concentrated' gives a better sense of its character than the more common 'intense', which is afflicted by a detritus of connotation deriving from Romantic philosophy, simple emotion and wayward individual personality; 'concentrated', too, better implies the masterful intelligence in disposition of words and meaning that governs good poetry. Further than this it should be said that the poem's concentration is an exacting discipline and framework designed to search out and convey an absolute truth: the truth must be absolute because only thus would the use of the most concentrated (and thus the highest, most human) of human forms of utterance be appropriately employed. But the process of concentrating meaning is, on each occasion, the work of a single human intelligence (whether the personality enters the work or not): thus each poem is unique. It is unique not only in execution, but in that it proceeds from a unique experience of life and it is the uniqueness of that experience that the poem has to, as part of its function, define.

The poem is thus *a concentrated account of the unique experience of the truth of an absolute truth*. (This is, of course, not the sole definition; it is a definition from the point of view of theory; for a definition from the point of view of the poet, see p. 34f.) The value of poetry as well as in its communicability lies in the absoluteness of the truth. That truth is objective, but objectivity would not be enough; thus one could not write a great poem *solely* on the objective truth that all men have only one head, unless one perceived behind that objectivity, the significance of the fact that all men had only one head (as that this was a design of their Creator). In the significance lies the absoluteness; in the objectivity lies the communication to the reader of the justice of the poet's hypothesis that his *unique* apprehension of *absolute* truth is applicable to all men. Apart from difference of talent the cultivation of uniqueness at the expense of absoluteness makes minor poetry, of uniqueness at the expense of objectivity, obscure poetry, and of uniqueness at the expense of concentration, bad poetry. Minor and obscure poetry is, of course, bad in relation to good poetry, but it is not wholly bad; only poetry that sets out to be unconcentrated is wholly bad, to the extent that it achieves its aim.

Objectivity is achieved by the ability of the poet to comprehend, sympathise with, understand and then judge ordinary human experience. The difficulty Lowell faced in the first phase of his career was that the simple truth that seemed to him absolute (the Puritan truth) was not easily related to human experience, as opposed to human intelligence. But it could be expressed overwhelmingly and powerfully: this enabled him to write a few short poems of the utmost concentration, complexity and power. The nature of the truth that most influenced him being once defined, however, it was destructive of poetry. If true, it was terrible and made all human experience insignificant, for it specifically denied communion with God who was its own fountain-head; in that sense, it made communication of and with itself impossible except through the technical rhetoric of poetry. A greater poet than Lowell might have held the balance longer or more effectively, perhaps through a qualification, perhaps unspoken, of the doctrine—Milton, who held the same view, nonetheless thought it worthwhile to justify the ways of God to man—but Lowell sought his way out in defences of obscurity, ambiguity and irony of temperament which could not, in the long run, satisfy his ambitions. Nonetheless, from its historical roots in the daily life of men, from the sanction given to the expounding of the doctrine in the works of Edwards and the Bible, from the tragic irony Lowell could express when comparing truth to the life of men, it was possible to write a limited amount of remarkable poetry. This tended to be denunciatory and all the denunciatory passages in 'The Quaker Graveyard' are Puritan.

To an extent not seen elsewhere, however—except in 'Colloquy in Black Rock', which is a special and not altogether pure example —'The Quaker Graveyard' sees Lowell as a Catholic poet, one whose Christianity is less specialised than the Puritan creed. The positive as opposed to the denunciatory passages of this poem are Christian mystical. This combination drives a deep fissure into the argument of the work. It has two other consequences in the poem, best explained in contrast to his Puritanism.

Historically rooted as it was, Lowell's doctrine, during the moments in which it was life-giving for his poetry, actually encouraged an explanation through human experience ('Mr. Edwards and the Spider') or through symbols traditionally expressing that experience in its religious aspect ('The Holy Innocents'). For reasons I will explain in a moment, his mysticism discouraged any such use of a human medium at the crisis in a poem. On the other hand, Lowell's Puritan doctrine was fierce; so terrible and all-encompassing was it that human experience was eventually all bound to seem of indistinguishable value and irrelevant before it. This was particularly so because, although ordinary life had to be lived, even in the presence of so formidable a faith, poetry does not have to be written; the concentration of poetry, combined with the consuming nature of the doctrine, tended to drive out what their fusion increasingly made irrelevant, that is the material of the poetry, human experience. In his inner self, however, Lowell was more committed to writing poetry than he was to the doctrine and so the devices spoken of earlier were used to conceal his dilemma. His mysticism, however, was a gentler doctrine, less terrifying, and allowing of a private, sustaining, exaltation. Consequently it allowed of a more elaborate explanation and approach; it was only when the centre of the doctrine—a point at which the Puritan influence could be at its best—was approached that its anti-poetic nature was revealed.

I shall, in a moment, speak of the many excellences of 'The Quaker Graveyard'. The crucial section is, however, section VI, the only one to be sub-titled ('Our Lady of Walsingham') and the one in which the themes of the poem are to be resolved. It is the most mystical section. I would, therefore, approach the task of analysis by resorting to the most comprehensive definition of Christian mysticism I have discovered, so that the reader will have this in mind as we work through the poem. Dom David Knowles writes:

> 'Mystical theology is thus distinguished both from what is called natural theology and from dogmatic and speculative theology. If by theology we mean the knowledge of God and his ways, it has always been the Christian teaching that we can have knowledge of God as our Maker and Governor by a natural process of reasoning; this is natural theology. To this we add what Jew and Christian have learned from scripture, and above all from the works and words of his Son, Jesus Christ . . . Beyond these kinds of knowledge there is a third by which God and the truths of Christianity can not only be believed and acted upon, but can in varying degrees be directly known and experienced . . . This knowledge, this experience, which is never entirely separable from an equally immediate and experimental union with God by love . . . *is totally incommunicable* [my italics], save as a bare statement, and in this respect all the utterances of the mystics are entirely inadequate as representation of the mystical experience, but it brings absolute certainly to the mind of the recipient.'[1]

We will see the effect of this definition in the climax of 'The Quaker Graveyard'.

The elegiac tradition is adhered to by Lowell in so far as it allows him to consider the meaning of Winslow's death and the evidence it offers for the elucidation—or at least definition—of more substantial and universal issues, described in an historical, a military and a cultural and religious background. Lowell manages to integrate into his text, not only words from Thoreau and Melville (as well as E. I. Watkins, of whom more later), but also his own idiosyncrasies of diction, particularly of transferred epithet and identity. The poem turns on an irony. The source of the irony is given in the legend at its head, 'Let man have dominion over the fishes of the sea and the fowls of the air and the beasts of the whole earth, and every creeping creature that moveth on the earth.' The irony is that, as the events of the poem demonstrate, men do not have that dominion, in the sense in which they understand it, that is, in the physical sense. This demonstration leads both to effects and conclusions. Principal among the effects is the way in which Lowell personalises and objectifies nature and the elements, giving more substance to fishes, sea, fowl, air, beasts and earth by placing them in the context of myth, classical and otherwise—Poseidon, who is the consort of Earth and hence Lord of Earthquakes, the most drastic of terrifying eruptions of nature, is the dominant presence—thus demonstrating that there is a deeper personality, a greater significance in the reaction of the elements to man's attempt to exercise his dominion.

There are many references to and borrowings from Melville in the poem. Principal among them are the lines in the third stanza:

> There, in the nowhere, where their boats were tossed
> Sky-high, where mariners had fabled news
> Of IS, the whited monster. What it cost
> Them is their secret.

Scrutinising this passage Mr. Staples pointed out its obvious nuances; its reference to the whale in *Moby Dick*; the fact that it will stand for the materialistic greed of the Quakers in the poem; and for both the Old and the New Testament God, the God of vengeance and of salvation and he gives also other nuances. With respect, however, my opinion is that the reference is more simple (directly to Melville) and more disciplined and encompassing: in *Moby Dick*, in his pursuit of the whale, Captain Ahab is attempting to exercise just that dominion over nature, *as misunderstood by man*, which is defined in the legend to 'The Quaker Graveyard'. His tragedy is that he senses his error, which is made explicit in the plight of his companions and the land-sea, known-unknown symbolism which runs through the novel. Lowell is thus deliberately making reference to and use of a modern myth-maker who defined the human dilemma in exactly the same way as Lowell does himself and who personalised and symbolised (in the sea generally and in the whale particularly) as well as deepening the meaning of the forces of nature against which man sets himself. The dilemma is the result of the failure of man to understand the message of God as expressed in the poem but, generally as set out in the legend. The particularity of identity which Lowell gives to natural forces is, technically speaking, set off by the particularity of identification Lowell gives to the human life in his poem by place names and history, in the same way, indeed, in which a remarkably particularised Nantucket is used in *Moby Dick* to represent the ordinary and secure life of men. The poet is present in the poem in the sense that it is he who describes the deeper identity of nature.

Thoreau is also much used in the poem and imagery from his *Cape Cod* dominates the first stanza. In my opinion he, the more conventionalised and stylised author, the victim at its loosest extreme of the incapacity to distinguish between the merit of different experiences and hence of the significance of experience at all, which could be the worst result of the Puritan doctrine of New England, is set off against Melville by Lowell. Into the first stanza, in which, as I say, the best part of the imagery is derived from Thoreau, Lowell injects the effect which I have been discussing, with its implication, of the personality of natural forces. This irony seems to me to be at the expense of Thoreau:

> A brackish reach of shoal off Madaket,—
> The sea was still breaking violently and night
> Had steamed into our North Atlantic Fleet,
> When the drowned sailor clutched the drag-net.

The phrase 'night/Had steamed . . .' is the personalisation I mean.
The first stanza is one of remarkable power and precision. As Lowell personalises both nature and inanimate objects, so he allows the depersonalisation of the corpse to assert itself: this is

directly from Thoreau and enhances the irony to be established later. 'The Quaker Graveyard' is far too long to allow of substantial quotations, however extended the analysis, but I will quote at large from the first stanza, to establish the tone of the poem within the context of my scrutiny:

> Light
> Flashed from his matted head and marbled feet,
> He grappled at the net
> With the coiled, hurdling muscles of his thighs:
> The corpse was bloodless, a botch of reds and whites,
> Its open, staring eyes
> Were lustreless dead-lights
> Or cabin-windows on a stranded hulk
> Heavy with sand.

Note the inner irony here, in which a corpse is allowed to appear to have life. Later, the stanza continues:

> Sailors, who pitch this portent at the sea
> Where dreadnoughts shall confess
> Its heel-bent deity,
> When you are powerless
> To sand-bag this Atlantic bulwark, faced
> By the earth-shaker, green, unwearied, chaste
> In his steel scales:

This is Poseidon, identified with earth and sea.

To resume my account of the argument of the poem. I have delineated some of the effects of the poem. Its conclusions are as follows. The attitude of man towards nature is the result of a misinterpretation by him of the words of God. The effect of nature upon him—nature's ability to kill—is proof of this misinterpretation. The misinterpretation truly lies, however, in man's behaviour, including his behaviour to other man. The appropriateness—the morality—of this argument as a reaction to the death of Winslow rests, as usual, on an unassailable fact—the ultimate impenetrability and the ultimate threat of nature, enriched by a complex but coherent symbolism. This part of the argument takes up the first five stanzas. The sixth, distinguished, as I have said, by a sub-title, gives the true message of God. The seventh is a coda, a summary and a contemporary warning, based on history.

As is common in Lowell's longer poems, the second stanza illustrates some of the themes of the first. Its power, scope and quality are undiminished, so it is necessary to point only to the way in which it carries forward the argument. In the first and second lines the winds 'are moving' and 'their breath/heaves'. The close terror of natural forces is driven home by Winslow's death 'In these home waters'; at this event the humbler creatures of nature 'tremble'; these are the terns and sea-gulls, over whom man supposedly has dominion and whose trembling suggests a greater power is at work and that man is mistaken in supposing, on the basis of the dominion given him in the passage from Genesis that he has true dominion over nature. Man's environment is here parti-cularised with the same sound effects as the terrifying marine scape that dominates the poem: the description is at once highly particularised and also enjoys the impression, beautifully conveyed, of being buffeted within a greater whole:

> Off 'Sconset, where the yawing S-boats splash
> The bellbuoy, with ballooning spinnakers,
> As the entangled, screeching mainsheet clears
> The blocks:

The stanza ends in a passage of great force which states the power of nature in relation to Winslow and concludes, by way of Mel-ville, with an account of the never-ending quest of some men for the meaning of the experience of the clash with nature symbolised by Ahab's pursuit of the whale and flawed by their desire for dominion: the irony in that flaw is conveyed by the fact that it is the bones which cry out

> The winds' wings beat upon the stones,
> Cousin, and scream for you and the claws rush
> At the sea's throat and wring it in the slush

> Of this old Quaker Graveyard where the bones
> Cry out in the long night for the hurt beast
> Bobbing by Ahab's whaleboats in the East.

The third stanza extends the argument to the contemporary world of the Second World War ('Our warships in the hand/of the great God') and backwards in time to the Quakers of New England. The poet does not know

> Whatever it was these Quaker sailors lost
> In the mad scramble of their lives.

Then, following the IS passage discussed above, Lowell summarises his theme in a passage of savage irony, famous and disputed:

> In the sperm-whale's slick
> I see the Quakers drown and hear their cry:
> 'If God himself had not been on our side,
> If God himself had not been on our side,
> When the Atlantic rose against us, why,
> Then it had swallowed us up quick.'

The telling word in this remarkably risky passage is 'quick'. It serves two facets of the same purpose. It is the poet who sees the drowning Quaker sailors; this is position as, so to speak, historian of the sailing epoch of New England. The meaning is that the Quaker affirmation had been used by the sailors throughout their lives and after occasions on which they had survived storms. Its use, however, showed their failure to appreciate the time-span within which nature worked: the Quakers took a temporary reprieve for a proof of God's special favour. The meaning is, however, telescoped and concentrated by juxtaposing the actual moment of fatality with all the other moments of escape, the repetition of which is conveyed by the repetition of the lines. The implication is thus that, with their lack of understanding the Quakers could not distinguish the fatal occasion when it arrived.

All this depends, of course, on the functioning of the poet's account of time, which is concentrated in the word 'quick'. The word, fitting the metrical scheme, is first used in a colloquial sense, as a natural expression of idiom. Thus used it encapsulates the dreadful irony—if the Atlantic has not swallowed them up 'quick' it swallowed them up 'slow'. Secondly, it sustains the poet's position as moral historian, for its significance can only be appreciated by him and that perception is uniquely conveyed in his prosodic structure. Thirdly, the word works backwards on the sense of time in the lines: it expresses the judgement that God's purpose works over a much greater time span than man appreciates—a mark, that, of the deficiency of his interpretation—and moves forward to the final line of the poem

> The Lord survives the rainbow of His will,

where 'rainbow' stands for 'appearance'.

These three stanzas complete the first movement of the poem. The second movement—Parts IV and V, the first consisting of two stanzas—contain the poet's reflections: in purpose and execution they are much inferior to what has gone before. The first stanza of Part V extends and generalises the argument and sees Lowell in a familiar vein of incantatory denunciation. His crudity is no longer contained ('To send the Pequod packing off to hell') and the stanza has a contemptuous, throwaway carelessness, unstiffened by the serious and particular thought that informed the first three. The second of the stanzas returns to sea and sailors; it implicitly contrasts the carelessness (in unjustified confidence) of the Quakers to the human cunning of Ulysses 'mast-lashed' to avoid being thrown into the sea in a storm, but to no particular point.

Part V, consisting of one stanza, continues the reflections, this time directed on the familiar theme of the corruption of the world, illustrated by the imagery of a whale hunt:

> When the whale's viscera go and the roll
> Of its corruption overruns this world

. . .
> The bones cry for the blood of the white whale,
> The fat flukes arch and whack about its ears,
> The death-lance churns into the sanctuary, tears
> The gun-blue swingle, heaving like a flail,
> And hacks the coiling life out:

The stanza ends

> Hide
> Our steel, Jonas Messias, in Thy side.

Mr. Staples suggests that this last line is a momentary consideration of salvation through Christ as a way out of the predicament,
the fierce invocation here to be answered by the peace of the
Virgin Mary in Part VI. The line is somewhat ambivalent and
might, indeed, bear that interpretation which, however, seems to
bear the corollary possible implication that Mary's Way is preferred to that of Jesus, which seems improbable. Another explanation seems to me more likely. The steel in the last line refers back
to the death-lance plunging into the whale and both refer to the
Roman soldier at the Crucifixion. With this interpretation the
last line can be made to bear a fruitful—and more typical
ambiguity: the steel, that is, all the condemned actions of man, are
hidden in God, that is, they are ultimately irrelevant to and
insignificant beside, his purpose; but, in hiding the steel in his
side, Jesus may also be pardoning man. This makes the last line of
Part V a potential, but not certain, source of hope, the nature of
which 'Our Lady of Walsingham' proceeds to delineate.

Though better than the stanzas of Part IV, Part V nonetheless
appears to me to illustrate some of the poem's deficiencies. Much
of the whale hunt imagery is gratuitous to the poem and relevant
only to itself: it does not have the concrete reality, that character
of assisting the argument forward that, say, the first stanza of all
does. Then, too, whatever may be made of my reading of the last
line, 'The death-lance churns into the sanctuary' cannot but be a
Crucifixion reference; as such it identifies the whale with Christ,
which in my view contradicts the IS reference, though Mr.

Staples maintains that IS may also be a reference to *Iesus Salvator*. That, indeed, is possible: it seems to me likely. But then the IS passage, the 'whited monster' cannot really bear any serious or direct Christian significance and can only suggest, in the dense overlay of symbols and references, that Lowell is uncertain about the relationship of the forces of nature and their mythologized expression, to God or, more properly, their function as instruments of God's will. If this is an honest doubt it is concealed beneath the overlay. Concealed, it diminishes the poet's authority for his claim, and the justification of his irony, is to a perception superior to that of the human sufferers.

The truth is that the complexity of possible relevance of the references, and of possible meanings of the symbols, obscures the failure to develop the central argument of the poem: there are too many possible meanings, the direction of which is uncontrolled and the weight of which is indecisively distributed. I have divided the central argument of the poem into its separate parts but I have barely touched (in discussing 'quick') on the overall interconnectedness of symbols thoughout the poem. For brevity, I will mention two of many. The portent pitched into the sea in the first stanza recalls the origin of life in the flux of the sea and calls up (in 'hell-bent deity') the possibility of re-disintegration; this is referred to again at the beginning of Part III ('All you recovered from Poseidon died/With you my cousin . . .') and again in the last stanza of all, Part VII, in the line 'When the Lord God formed man from the sea's slime'. The second interconnected symbol is bones, the meaning of which I discussed for the second stanza, Part II, and which recurs in the first (directly) and the second (implicitly) stanzas of Part IV, again in Part V and is related (in the same way as in 'Colloquy in Black Rock') to the slime and sea symbols already mentioned and brought together with them in the very last stanza.

This interpenetration of the structure of the poem gives it an altogether illusory strength. For the general life-from-slime imagery has a general truth, is given, in the beginning of Part III, a particular and not elsewhere justified reference to Winslow and is put, finally, into another ambivalent relationship in the very last stanza, through which the whole relationship between God and the forces of nature is thrown in doubt again:

> And breathed into his face the breath of life,
> And blue-lung'd combers lumbered to the kill.

I have only touched on these ambiguities and hints. To explore them thoroughly—the various significances or possible significances of 'blue' for instance—would fill my entire book with a discussion of this poem alone. I do not believe discussion would be greatly advanced by the relentless pursuit of such—once the structure is established—easily contrived reverberations to none of which the poet is decisively committed. Later (on p. 129f) I discuss the relative characters of positive and negative ambiguity. For the moment it is enough to say that positive ambiguity shows control by the artist over—and often though not always decision between —a range of experiences and judgements. In the remarkable passage in Jane Austen's *Emma* in which Emma discovers Knightley loves her, a whole series of different lines of knowledge, experience, awareness of life and its spiritual and moral meaning are rapidly traced outwards from Emma by the author; the whole is controlled and comprehended—resolved—as one experience, but the different lines are discriminated between while their fusion in the whole makes up an untranslatable and ultimately mysterious intimation of truth. The passages are too long to quote here, but a part of a sentence gives a critical account of the phenomenon:

> 'While he spoke, Emma's mind was most busy, and, with all the wonderful velocity of thought, had been able—and yet without losing a word—to catch and comprehend the exact truth of the whole;'

That 'velocity of thought' is precisely what Lowell needs to achieve in this complex poem—no better description could be devised—and it is also precisely what close inspection shows him to have failed to achieve. Nonetheless, passages in the poem are remarkable and the effect of this failure on the whole remains to be assessed by reference to Lowell's own resolution.

'Our Lady of Walsingham' consists of two stanzas. Their phraseology is largely derived from E. I. Watkins' *Catholic Art and Culture*. The first stanza sets a peaceful pastoral scene. Lowell introduces his sailor to it, conveying that 'by that stream' the water, destructive elsewhere in the poem, is tamed. The peace, however, is merely human, it is the ambience of the penitents in the first line. Gently, with 'But see' in the last line, the poet, mediating again in the poem, guides the sailor away from human peace to the real truth. I shall quote the whole of the second stanza:

> Our Lady, too small for her canopy,
> Sits near the altar. There's no comeliness
> At all or charm in that expressionless
> Face with its heavy eyelids. As before,
> This face, for centuries a memory,
> *Non est species, neque decor,*
> Expressionless, expresses God: it goes
> Past castled Sion. She knows what God knows,
> Not Calvary's Cross nor crib at Bethlehem
> Now, and the world shall come to Walsingham.

I have already (above, p. 17) set down my animadversions on this crucial passage. Suffice it to note here how, in the last three lines, Lowell devalues not only human grandeur (castles) and the facts of birth and death but the traditional and particular Christian formulations, especially of the last two, which establish a relationship between man and God. He claims here, in flat, expressionless lines, the incommunicability of the mystic, discussed earlier in this chapter, which is not the same thing as saying that he *is* a mystic or that we are obliged to entertain, let alone believe, his message. This is the vice of imitative form, in which the poet tries to convey meaning by making his lines reflect exactly the appearance of things rather than express the meaning to which his perception guides him. The imitation here is in no way rescued by the final stanza, which reviews the experience of the poem and ends with a more resonant expression of the same statement

> The Lord survives the rainbow of His will.

'The Quaker Graveyard' is one of the most praised of Lowell's poems partly, no doubt, because its ambition and scope is taken for an extension of the quality generally, if falsely, found in his shorter poems. It has passages of distinct and considerable power. The augument, expressed without the ambiguities, is tenable, appropriate and elevating and the first three stanzas or Parts are a fine achievement in themselves. The difficulty and the fault of the whole design lies, of course, in the failure of its resolution and, though to a lesser extent, in the failure of Parts IV, V and VII. The extent of the flaw is materially increased by what I have called the 'interpenetration' of the structure with ambiguously evaluated symbolic nuances. The *argument*, considered narrowly, is resolved at least theoretically (let us leave aside the quality of the resolution); but the symbolic pattern, which is part of the argument, considered broadly, is not.

The continual appearance of and stress on, not only the nuances, but the range of their possible meanings and references force the whole early part of the poem into the mould of an introduction. The expectation is naturally, and properly, aroused that there will be a final and comprehensive statement of meaning. Now, an introductory character of this kind is not at all unusual in Lowell. 'Mr. Edwards and the Spider' might be considered entirely as an introduction to the last line and without that line the poem as a whole would be inconsiderable. In 'The Quaker Graveyard' the introduction introduces nothing; the unsatisfactory nature of 'Our Lady at Walsingham' as a resolution may, indeed, have prompted the final stanza, which is in a more characteristic mode of finalisation. Except through the re-appearance of symbolism, however, the final stanza offers nothing comprehensive of the poetic nature of the argument.

The doctrine and definition of Christian mysticism cannot be blamed, any more than New England Puritanism, elsewhere for Lowell's failure, but the doctrine itself is not conducive nor encouraging to poetry. Like the other, it is a framework within which, saving superior talent, the capacity to live with the concentrated expression of poetry as other men live with daily life, while assenting to a draconian conviction, only a temporary balance is likely. It must also be said, however, the measure of success this large design achieves may be in part due to the smaller strain mysticism imposed on Lowell. Part VI is separate from the rest of the conception; it ruins the resolution, but it does not corrupt the earlier stanzas, as his Puritanism sometimes does in other poems and, indeed as its remains do here. Finally, for Lowell himself it must be said that the intervention of the poet here is of a more traditional kind, an intervention as moral historian. It works well for a time on that level and only close inspection reveals the weakness of decision in the operation. Nonetheless that particular weakness of Lowell's characteristic personal intervention is concealed in 'The Quaker Graveyard'.

'The Mills of the Kavanaughs' is Lowell's longest poem: for him, its thirty-eight stanzas represent a unique effort. Like all the poems in the volume to which it gives the title, 'The Mills of the Kavanaughs' represents a departure by Lowell from his Christian and overtly Catholic concerns of the earlier period. Objective evidence of the deliberation of this move in the case of this long poem is provided by the excision of Catholic symbolism from *The Kenyon Review* version of the title poem before publication of the volume.

The new basis of the poem is the myth of Persephone and Pluto. In the myth Persephone, the daughter of Demeter, is sent by Jupiter to join Aidoneus in Hades. After a long agitation Demeter secures her return, on condition that Persephone resided on earth for three months of the year. This compromise enabled the earth to bring forth fruit again, after an interruption of the agricultural cycle by Demeter. The meaning of the myth, then, is that Persephone is the seed corn; she remains concealed in the ground for part of the year and, on her return to her mother, is the corn which nourishes life on earth.

In the poem the action takes place in 1943. Anne, widow of Harry Kavanaugh, sits alone in the garden of her declining home,

4*

recalling her marriage, the war service and subsequent madness of her husband; his attempt to kill her and his suicide. The poem combines description of the present with reverie about the past, and the borders between the two are mixed and overlapping. All the action takes place within Anne's imagination and the reverie, analogous to the seasons, covers four periods of her life; childhood and courtship are succeeded by marriage which is unhappy and unsuccessful, partly because of Harry's madness and partly because her idealization of him has made it impossible for her to live with and comfort the real man.

I do not intend to discuss this poem in detail. Mr. Staples gives an excellent general account of its meaning and Mr. Dudley Fitts an appreciative if ultimately reserved critical account.[2] It exhibits all the ambiguities of meaning and nuances of symbolism that we have seen in 'The Quaker Graveyard' but to a much greater extent; the resources of Ovid's *Metamorphoses* are called upon by Lowell; and the central ambivalence lies in the character of Anne herself, contradictory in all things, even in alternate attachments to life and death, as is appropriate to her origin in the myth. Multiple allusions are created, to other myths as well as to other poets until the poem is clogged, not with judgements, but with references:

> The children whisper. Old and pedastalled,
> Where rock-pools used to echo when she called
> Demeter—sheathed in Lincoln green, a sheaf—
> The statue of Persephone regards
> The river, while it moils a hundred yards
> Below her garland. Here, they used to build
> A fire to broil their trout. A beer can filled
> With fish skins marks the dingle where they died.
> They whisper, 'Touch her. If her foot should slide
> A little earthward, Styx will hold her down
> *Nella miseria*, smashed to plaster, balled
> Into the whirlpool's boil.'

This passage, and particularly *Nella miseria* from Dante, has given rise to disputation; Mr. Staples finds it acceptable and justifiable and Mr. Fitts does not. The real difficulty with a poem such as this, which carries to an extreme a tendency to reference found almost everywhere in Lowell, lies not in the appropriateness or inappropriateness of particular references or images but in the structure of the work as a whole.

The underlying contemporary structure of 'The Mills of the Kavanaughs' is easy to discern. It is a lament for and a meditation on the decline and imminent fall of an old house and an old family. The tragedy of the family is partly revealed and partly distorted by the ironic ambivalence of Anne, the woman adopted into the family and married to its son, who should have but cannot bring with her the fertility of life she is supposed to represent and her representation of which is given substance by the basic analogy to the myth of Persephone. Persephone's life is, however, eternal and her cycle ever-recurring. Anne is human and, like Harry, the Kavanaughs and their house (called *Kavanaugh*) will decline and die. By perceiving the analogy, however, Anne is enabled to perceive also an actual similarity to Persephone, an intimation, as it were, of immortality or at least uniqueness of experience. This enables Anne, in some passages of dignity and great sadness, to accept her fate by the wisdom she has achieved through suffering and intelligent perception, a wisdom that encompasses death and ruin as well as the influence of her own divided personality on their production:

> There, a maternal nineteenth century
> Italian statue of Persephone
> Still beckons to a mob of Bacchanals
> To plunge like dogs or athletes through the falls,
> And fetch her the stone garland she will hurl.
> The lady drops her cards. She kneels to furl
> Her husband's flag, and thinks his mound and stone
> Are like a buried bed. 'This is the throne
> They must have willed us. Harry, not a thing
> Was missing: we were children of a king.

Once that main line of development is established, however, the symbolism and allusions do not advance the argument: they merely decorate the phenomenon. The structure of Lowell's impressionism is loose and a mystic aura is created by the multitude of reference. Much of that reference, however, is pseudo, in that the symbolic values alluded to—and, indeed, the reader is invited to choose for himself between them—are present greatly in excess of the rational coherence of the poem. To an extent, the multiplicity of reference, particularly to myths which supposedly themselves symbolise perennial truths experienced by man, creates an impression of rather loosely erudite universality, and some readers may find this adequate to their taste. Decoration, however, rather than concentration, is the overall achievement of the poem and its overlapping myths are more in the nature of a contrived effect—despite, as always with Lowell, passages of beauty—than a lived and judged experience. Chasing down the ramifications of meaning in the references may be, as Mr. Staples says, a challenge to the intelligence, but it is so to the detective rather than the critical intelligence and it results in a thin spreading, rather than a concentration of knowledge and experience: allusiveness, however elaborate, is not poetry.

'The Mills of the Kavanaughs' appears to have come, for Lowell, between Christianity and the personal explorations of *Life Studies*. In this interim period the classics, which have always had a dual use for him in that, in the myth they enshrine, they testify to truths of experience so continually apprehended as to attain a near-absolute character, while they are also a facet of the contemporaneity of history, became dominant in his work. The myth here, and its ramifications, assisted length in the poem, as did his increasingly horrified explorations of sanity and insanity which dominates 'The Mills of the Kavanaughs'. It was as though, losing something hitherto central, Lowell tried to use with full force all that he was certain remained. The result is rich, but opaque and decadent. It was, however, only an interim.

4 Life Studies

IT IS ALWAYS difficult (and dangerous, too) to divide Lowell too
readily into periods. *Lord Weary's Castle, Land of Unlikeness* and
The Mills of the Kavanaughs encapsulate, at least in embryo, not
only the major themes of his life's work, but the variations he has
played on these themes as well. Thus, the reader who is familiar
with Lowell's early work in the most convenient, if incomplete,
compendium (*Poems 1938–49*), will be familiar also with the nature
and contradictions of his view of his Boston heritage: they are all
summarised in 'In Memory of Arthur Winslow'. There are, in
the earlier work, even some hints of the kind of personal involvement and analysis central to the last four poems of *Life Studies*,
'Memories of West Street and Lepke', 'Man and Wife', 'To
speak of the woe that is in marriage' and 'Skunk Hour'.
Nonetheless, *Life Studies* was a major departure.

The departure was to be seen, not in any tremendous
psychological transformation of Lowell (as has been implied) but
in his abandonment of the highly developed formal structures
that had hitherto been integral to his thought and performance as
a poet. It still perhaps requires a certain effort of mind truly to
integrate form with matter in thought about poetry: nonetheless
that is what one must do if one is to appreciate the significance of
Lowell's abandonment of the formalism he had so rigidly and
assiduously cultivated as far as *Life Studies*.

The essence of Lowell's earlier forms (efficiently noted by
Allen Tate in his introduction to *Land of Unlikeness* and by Mr.
Hugh Staples in *Robert Lowell: The First Twenty Years*) was, I
believe, that they were the bedrock of authority from which he
spoke his poetic judgements on the world. The Catholic Church
he had chosen, as a framework of belief, faith and judgement:
New England was in his bones and he could not, as a public poet,
avoid it. The essential contemporaneity of all history—a concept

that can be described and used only poetically—was his most essential insight. Form was, firstly, the way in which these materials and this insight could be transmuted and, secondly, the essential curb on his violent spirit, while being also the alchemist's store, the badge of his authority.

The real agent of synthesis, of course, was not religion, nor New England, nor historical insight, nor form, but Lowell's own uncurbable personality. Religion, as his mixture of Puritanism and Catholicism shows, was in true fact, not for him an ordered system of moral reference but a concatenation of symbolisms with which he could elaborately decorate a single proposition—the ruination of man—which was a product of the way Lowell saw God rather than the way in which he received God's message. One of his greatest triumphs in religious poetry, 'The Holy Innocents', was a triumph of a technique rather, as much as of poetic insight. New England was an experience, personal and cultural, that nagged at him as at an open wound: it was something he was compelled to deal with, but which gave him little positive support, again, on the evidence as much because of his personality as because of the deficiencies of New England itself. Insight and form together were often used as a technique of evasion rather than a method of achievement. The energy spent on words—as Mr. Ian Hamilton said in a delightful phrase,—'seems bent on increasing their volume without sharpening their point'. Thus, in spite of considerable triumphs, the early work was seriously flawed. Too much—in terms of the intractability of the material—had been demanded by Lowell of himself as a solvent. Instead, however, of going under to the demands and dictates of any one or some of the elements in his early work Lowell went about instead on the other tack: he stripped his personality almost bare of what had been at once his protective foliage and his dominating subject matter and tried to let it stand alone in direct relation to his experience. What happened was not a fundamental reformation of personality so much as a simple redirection, which may have had traumatic origins and certainly had tremendous consequences.

It would also be a fallacy to suppose that *Life Studies* represented

any radical change in Lowell's character as a public poet: the placing of him, with this volume, in the 'confessional' school was
both mistaken and misleading, though it revealed an essential
part of the way in which Lowell, and the critics and commenta-
tors who admire him, thought about their—and man's—place in
the world of affairs. The presumption in the identification of
Lowell with, say, Sylvia Plath—and Rosenthal included him in his
list of confessional poets—was essentially that value in the world
of public affairs, the quality of the life of politics and society, is
mirrored in the private psychological state of man and particularly of the artist. This is not in itself an ignoble or self-
evidently untrue proposition. But it is one the logic of which, as
well as its implications for poetry, had to be examined and faced.
If P. H. Newby is right, the road to this proposition began in the
Second World War, the horrors of which deprived writers in
English (and perhaps their culture) of a framework of broadly
acceptable moral values and references: I hope to show, however,
that the whole process goes much further back—though climactic
points may be plotted with fair accuracy—though my purpose of
the moment is merely to define the present state of things.

   More often than not, of course, Lowell refuses to commit himself simply or crudely or openly to the idea that the individual
phsychological state represents the truth about the world. There
is a reserve, an ambiguity, about his position. Nonetheless, the
idea influences him and that influence is most marked in the
course of the psychological trauma of *Life Studies*:

> These are the tranquillized *Fifties*,
> and I am forty. Ought I to regret my seedtime?
> I was a fire-breathing Catholic C.O.,
> and made my manic statement,
> telling off the state and president, and then
> sat waiting sentence in the bull pen
> beside a negro boy with curlicues
> of marijuana in his hair.

The poem from which this extract comes—'Memories of West
Street and Lepke'—is far from straightforward. One of the points

to notice instantly about it—and this is a point to bear in mind throughout any reading of *Life Studies*—is the extent to which it is *not* straightforward. It—and the volume—is far from the simple, courageous baring of soul and psyche that the term 'confessional' poetry is meant to imply; it is, indeed, both courageous and a baring of the soul—occasionally quite frighteningly so, as in 'Skunk Hour'—but it is far from simple and direct. If Lowell left his protective covering behind with the rich forms and elaborate themes of *Poems 1938-49*, he did not leave behind either his ambiguity or his evasion.

In the passage just quoted, in the third and fourth lines, Lowell —referring to an autobiographical incident—suddenly questions his whole earlier poetic practice. But the hint here that he might have been wrong is also a hint that he might simply have been ineffective. For the obvious and recorded move from earlier beliefs and practices does not induce in Lowell any hint that earlier judgements might have been wrong: he is still after the same public targets. The point is illustrated by another passage from 'West Street and Lepke', with its scornful judgement in the tail:

> where even the man
> scavenging filth in the back alley trash cans,
> has two children, a beach wagon, a helpmate,
> and is a 'young Republican'.

This is good swingeing stuff, but it is at best Charles Churchill. At a deeper level it is profoundly disappointing from a man with the ambition and ability of Lowell. Viewing the poem (and it is representative of the volume) in the perspective of Lowell's career, one cannot allow that he has established his authority to abandon the form and the system of belief so integral to his early work and still maintain the total validity of the judgement on man originally divined through the medium of the now discredited apparatus. Within the context of the first passage of 'West Street and Lepke' quoted one cannot allow that Lowell has established his authority to retain unvarnished the judgement in the second quotation when he is dealing so contemptuously with his own capacity to judge ('telling off state and president' and placing himself in the humiliating position described). And if it is maintained that the stanza of self-contempt quoted means, not that Lowell is being self-contemptuous but that, in the last six lines, he is judging his tormentors ironically, by seeing himself partly through their eyes, one can only say that, though the hypothesis is admissible, its validity cannot with certainty be established; and so neither can the consequent hypothesis which must follow, that *Life Studies* is a courageous change of tactics, be established. The truth is that, though I prefer my own reading, the stanza is at best ambiguous; and though ambiguity of a high order is a necessary element in poetry, it here represents evasion. Despite the desperate change of course, the new style of *Life Studies* conceals the recurrent inability of Lowell to find resources for judgement; hopefully, it conceals also Lowell's awareness of this inability. But the fact of the matter is that a public poet must judge and, when doing so, he must demonstrate the authority of his judgement. In *Life Studies*, the private psychology of Robert Lowell is, at the bottom, a simulacrum of that authority: private man reflects public chaos.

Some of the critical quotations in the first chapter of this book —notably that from Elizabeth Bishop—show in outline the character of the moral disintegration of the judging intelligence that is featured in Lowell's work (though the work sometimes triumphs over it) and which so frequently marks commentary on his poetry. It seems clear that one of the major influences on this psychological development has been the more brutal facts of modern history. In an interview with Professor Donald Davie, Mr. A. Alvarez, one of Lowell's most enthusiastic admirers, made some observations about the state of modern poetry. He pointed out that, in his view, 'most of the really important writers' of the past had been 'on the Right' but that 'since the rise and fall of the Third Reich' such an alignment was no longer possible. I do not know what Mr. Alvarez means by 'on the Right', unless it be admittedly merely a vague and instinctive generalisation; but he tried to explain why he saw the political alignment as no longer possible for writers:

'There is a poem by Marianne Moore, "On Poetry", which begins "I, too, dislike it. There are things important beyond all this fiddle."[2] It seems to me that what happened in Auschwitz, and the other 130 concentration camps that were within the Reich, and that's happening in concentration camps in Russia and presumably in China and so on, is of an order that makes it very very important to, as it were, be sane about one's own identity, to be sure about one's own identity, because the whole movement of the concentration camps is the movement to destroy individuals, and towards the kind of efficiency that destroys art. One has simply got to say that the seeds of the concentration camps are in us all—we've all got these self-destructive tendencies, tendencies not to give up the fight, but simply to hand over your identity. And you can do it in all sorts of ways; you can do it in your personal life, you can do it in your working life. But to use the immortal words of E. E. Cummings: "There is some shit I will not eat." That is absolutely vital. One has got to be able to cope with one's society—its traps and shams.'[1]

There is nothing apocalyptic or moving about this particular outburst of discontent: certainly there is nothing in it either intellectually or emotionally appropriate to the moral challenge (of Auschwitz) to which Mr. Alvarez claims to be reacting. Yet, this kind of 'thinking' is more than common in literary comment today. It, as I said in my first chapter, breaks out like a rash in critical reviews whenever a new volume by Lowell appears. Mr. Cyril Connolly's comment on the poems in Near the Ocean— 'each of them near perfect in their gravel-voiced despair', a phrase in which 'despair' is used as a word of praise—is an example of the syndrome.

Now, I do not want to be unfair either to the feelings or to the capacity of Lowell's critics. Nor do I want to confuse them with him: his thought and accomplishment is very nearly always superior in quality to what is written about him. What I am trying to define is the intellectual ambience that surrounds him, the characteristics of which his work, whether against his will or not, encourages. Few would, I think, deny, that the mood most sanctioned in contemporary literature is of despair and dissatisfaction. It is, moreover, a particularly *public* despair, a *public* dissatisfaction, as Mr. Alvarez's references to Auschwitz and concentration camps, and the references of others (including Lowell) to Vietnam and nuclear war, as well as a multitude of other subjects, show. It rests, further, on the conviction felt that there is an organic relationship between the activity of literature and the activities of men. More precisely, the mood stands for the belief that the practice of men—in our time what writers and critics alike feel to be the numbingly inhuman practice of man—has a direct and immediate relevance to the practice of literature. I would like to hazard further: it seems to me that the intimacy writers and critics alike feel between art and events is more pronounced now, and more moving, more a moral —that is, a judging—intimacy than for many generations past.

That, it seems to me, is a fair statement of the case, a fair description of the way many artists and critics feel about the contemporary situation. Whether one agrees or disagrees with the particular general diagnosis seems to me to be irrelevant. From the point of view of the criticism of literature, moreover, the accuracy or inaccuracy of the particular facts of the diagnosis— unless they intrude organically into literature itself—is also irrelevant. It is irrelevant, further, to challenge the phenomenon by some statement such as that poets and artists do not understand the issues of real life. The real issue is the quality of the artistic response to the diagnosis.

The real nature of that response can be effectively defined theoretically and, as with the first phase of Lowell's career, though the theoretical analysis does not dominate the poetic practice it influences it and, in my view, generally mars it. What Lowell has done in *Life Studies* is to try to put his personality into direct relationship with experience, without the mediating agents and resources available to him in his first phase, particularly, without religion and, frequently, without a controlling form. The effect of the absence of form was noted by Mr. Hamilton in the essay I have already referred to. He compared a passage from Lowell's prose essay '91 Revere Street',

'Almost immediately he [Lowell's father] bought a largerand more stylish house; he sold his ascetic stove-black Hudson and bought a plump brown Buick; later the Buick was exchanged for a high-toned, as-good-as-new Packard with a custom-designed royal blue and mahogany body. Without drama, his earnings more or less decreased from year to year'.

with a poem on exactly the same subject ('Commander Lowell')

> whenever he left a job,
> he bought a smarter car.
> Father's last employer
> Was Scudder, Stevens and Clarke, Investment Advisers,
> himself his only client.
> While Mother dragged to bed alone,
> Read Menninger,
> and grew more and more suspicious,
> he grew defiant.
> Night after night,
> *à la clarté déserte de sa lampe,*
> he slid his ivory Annapolis slide rule
> across a pad of graphs—
> piker speculations! In three years
> he squandered sixty thousand dollars.

and comments

'There is no reason why the first of these passages should be set out as prose and the second syntactically line-broken into verse: indeed, the first passage acts on the reader more "poetically"—that is, the colours and the car—names are allowed to do the work and there is none of the chattiness that distends the second. The closing comments on Father's earnings could be interchanged without loss either way.'

The dissolution of form is not the whole story; and it does not take place everywhere in *Life Studies*. It derives, however, from the nature of the response to experience we are discussing and its partial abandonment by Lowell is an important pointer to the emotional principles underlying that response.

The closer the direct relationship between the personality and the experience the weaker and less weighty is the personality as a judging element. It is worth noting, in the quotation from Mr. Alvarez above, that a direct relationship is established between concentration camp and individual personality. As far as it goes, this statement is, of course, precisely true. But it is not the concentration camp that is the object of Mr. Alvarez's attack: that object (if I understand him aright) is, rather, the working out of the potential of 'these self-destructive tendencies' he claims we all have inside us in a situation in which one is tempted 'to hand over your identity' to a society full of 'traps and shams'. Mr. Alvarez does not, that is, fear (or fear immediately) the establishment of concentration camps in the Home Counties; rather, desperately moved by the camps, he insists that, anti-personality and anti-individuality as they are, they represent in its most terrible form a basic threat of depersonalisation in modern society. Presumably (though I do not certainly know this) Mr. Alvarez would maintain that the American intervention in Vietnam is the completion of the circle, in that here modern society has gone to work in a fashion that has caused intelligent men and women to recall the bestialities of Nazi Germany: certainly the circle has been completed in this way by others.

We may presume all men share the attitude of Mr. Alvarez to the concentration camps. As to whether the seeds of destruction lie within all of us and as to whether his view of society as a bed of 'traps and shams' is true, most of us would require more evidence. That evidence need not be mathematical proof of the proposition: poets and critics are not politicians, psychiatrists or soothsayers. The evidence must lie in quality of response: a quality of response which demonstrates the authority of Mr. Alvarez (or whoever) to make the diagnosis. It is this quality which is missing from the quotation above, and from the quotations from Miss Bishop and Mr. Pearson in Chaper One. It is also missing from most of the poems in *Life Studies*.

Implicit, of course, in Mr. Alvarez's remarks is a further proposition: that, in analysing the dread of our times, more than a mere or ordinary personality is involved; it is, rather, the response of the artist or critic, or the artist as critic, that is at issue. In respect of Lowell, the same is surely true: it is not merely an ordinary— or just any—personality he wants to put in contact with experience, but the personality of an artist. Precisely viewed, therefore, the attempt in *Life Studies* is to put the individual personality directly in contact with experience with as few mediating agents as are possible or *necessary to continue to write poetry*. Implicity, the authority of the statement lies in the quality of the poetry or, in the case of Mr. Alvarez's statement above, the quality of the thought. In other words, art is important.

My view of the history of the direct intervention of the poet in the poem was set out in Chapter One. From what I said there it will be clear that I do not believe personal intervention as such to be a bad thing; it will be clear, however, that I take it to represent a decline, since it is in some way an attempt to close the gap in an argument by weight of personal feeling, an interpretation of cultural resources no longer being enough; it will be nonetheless also clear that, in my opinion, very great poetry can still be written in this mode, provided a balance is maintained between personality and resources. The less personality however (in general terms), the more objectivity (artistic, not scholarly) and the better the poem. This does not, of course, mean, say, that all sixteenth-century poetry is better than all eighteenth-century poetry; or that all eighteenth-century poetry is better than all twentieth-century poetry. Ultimately, even objective poetry is written by an individual with talent. Though the conditions for writing poetry may be better in the sixteenth than the eighteenth and in the eighteenth than the twentieth, century, the talent in the later may be superior to the talent in the earlier, periods. One of the duties of the critic is to help the poet understand the limiting conditions of his period. The difficulty of the poet is to overcome these conditions by understanding them.

Unless Mr. Alvarez believes that the essence of his argument is that anybody can make it with equal authority (which is anarchy in which art has no place) he believes that art is important. If it is important it must have quality of mind and moral feeling. If it has these it must be able to discriminate between experience, comprehend and control them and, finally, judge them. If all these qualities are present in criticism or in art (though good criticism is inferior to good art its aims are the same) the kind of woolly statement I quoted from Mr. Alvarez could not be made, for it is a statement wholly lacking in discrimination or strength of judgement. It matters not, I repeat, whether the proposition he makes is true or not (I do not believe it is): what matters is the failure to discriminate between a series of events and experiences, between different kinds of evidence. The presence of discrimination is itself evidence of quality of mind. Commonsense indicates that all the situations described by Mr. Alvarez are not the same, therefore it behoves him to discriminate between them. Finally, since Mr. Alvarez has elsewhere shown at least a general ability to appreciate quality,[2] one must assume that his is not a failure of intelligence but of doctrine, whether wholly understood or not.

The difficulty of attempting to judge experience by personality is to know how much of the mediating agencies of form, religion or system of belief to dispense with and when to do so. Implicit in the doctrine, however, is a tendency to dispense with mediation altogether. But personality and personal judgement are not agents of discrimination: discrimination comes from education, experience, understanding of humanity and, to some extent, an appreciation of values lying outside the individual—of values objective, permanent, religious, social or political, but in some way moral or immutable. To the extent that one rests on the personality *tout entière* discrimination becomes difficult and then impossible. To the extent that discrimination disappears, judgement is valueless, because there are no standards of judgement. To that extent all experience is the same, and even a statement to the effect that our individuality is worth defence has no objective support: it is the huddling together of animals in the darkness of primeval night for at least the comforts of miserable togetherness. If all this is true, art is valueless, because its morality is founded in psychological whim rather than immutable value: since, however, the experience of life delineated is unhappy, the doctrine is not hedonistic. It can properly be called inverse hedonism. Nonetheless, it derives from the hedonism entering English literature with

Romantic self-expression and finding its most comprehensive formulation in Walter Pater. Its ultimate implication is the doctrine of the valuelessness of both art and judgement, and the exaltation of indifferent instinct.

Let us look at the first poem in *Life Studies* in the light of these general remarks. 'Beyond the Alps' is the poem in which Lowell specifically announces his departure from religion. It is one of four poems published between 1953 and 1954. The third stanza did not appear in the first (English) edition of *Life Studies* but was contained in the (English) edition of *For the Union Dead*. It was restored, with emendations, in the second English edition of *Life Studies*.

'Beyond the Alps' takes the outward form of a journey from Rome to Paris. Though the form of the poem—each stanza is a rhyming semi-sonnet—is greatly relaxed as compared to his earlier work, metrical and syntactical order is maintained. The outward metaphor of a journey, however, allows Lowell to mix disparate symbols and images in an apparently disordered fashion, miming the motion of the journey, its jolting and the ascent and descent of the Alps. Apart, however, from being ordered within the outward, anecdotal framework of History, the images form another, more philosophical pattern: they invariably symbolise aspects of man's condition; the jumble and disorder of the journey, with its changing speeds and directions, reflects a more basic disorder of nature, a disorder of impulse, aspiration and action; that disorder is itself a metaphor; within it the placing of each image is significant and deliberate. The first question, therefore, is the nature of the meaning the metaphors reflect.

In the light of the theoretical discussion above, I want to emphasise two points that come across immediately from the text. In the first stanza, referring first to Rome, Lowell shifts to Mussolini:

> There the skirt-mad Mussolini unfurled
> the eagle of Caesar. He was one of us
> Only, pure prose.

In other words, there is in each of us the tendency to corruption and power-mania Lowell sees in Mussolini—the seeds of destruction are within us all. The question then is, what is the differentiation between us and Mussolini that the lines imply?

I shall return to this point in a moment. Just now I want to pursue the ironic deflation implied in the action of Mussolini unfurling the legions of Caesar. By the restoration of the originally omitted stanza, Lowell has reduced that irony:

> Rome asked for poets. At her beck and call,
> Came Lucan, Tacitus and Juvenal,
> the *black republicans* who tore the tits
> and bowels of the Mother Wolf to bits.
> Killer and army-commander waved the rod
> of empire over the Caesars' salvaged bog . . .

In *For the Union Dead* 'Then psychopath and soldier' was in place of 'Killer and army-commander': this restored stanza is crucial to the poem, but I want to point out here only the fact that, in it, the Caesars are placed in the same barbaric bracket as Mussolini.

The destructiveness of man—and his self-destructiveness—are thus established. The second point is to note the starting point of the poem, its vantage point as it were: no longer is there an attempt to objectify the statement. Now, in the first stanza, we are told, with the personal pronoun, that it is the poet himself who is undertaking to explain the journey through life and from faith:

> Much against my will,
> I left the City of God where it belongs.

The poet is introduced thus into a direct relationship with experience, and must bear that burden. Moreover, with 'Much against my will', Lowell establishes that he has unwillingly left the consolations of faith, and this adds to the claim of authority he is making for himself alone.

Thus the preliminaries. I now want to make some general observations about the poem which form the substance of my judgement on it, before trying to substantiate that general judgement from the text. This is a poem of discontent, dismay and disillusion. Its most obvious weapon is an extremely crude and vulgar (in thought and expression) irony. The appearance of that irony deceives, for what the poet tries to do with it is convict by implication. Irony is a stylistic instrument of satire, which points to a weakness in the object of attack. Authority and discrimination is therefore required to select the point of weakness. What Lowell does with the instrument here is, not exploit a weakness, but use irony for a full-scale frontal assault, for which anger, not irony, is the appropriate instrument. Irony, however, has this advantage for Lowell: its local characteristics distract attention from the role it plays in the poem, from its place in the structure of judgement the poem represents. It is not, therefore, always apparent to what degree the poet is committed to the attack implicit in the irony, though the logic of his position compels a full commitment. Lowell thus, by his use of irony, conceals what he is saying and allows the part to stand for the whole and the appearance for the reality, while he defines, at crucial points, only the appearance, not the reality. At the same time his other devices of analogy and juxtaposition—and his belief in the contemporaneity of history—from the earlier phase of his career, are used to create a structure of ambiguity, through which the person is encouraged to take a despairing view of affairs: the poet, however, is not committed finally to that particular analysis, but only to the general view of affairs, to the general mood established. Even when he encourages a positive inclination, against the grain of his diagnosis, he does not commit himself to it. It seems to me therefore, that Lowell cannot come to judgement through discrimination and that he knows he cannot. Instead, however, of writing a poem of honest doubt and feeling, he has written a poem of judgement, because it is his ambition to do so: the poem is thus both self-willed and self-indulgent. It is evasive and self-concealing. When evasion and judgement are combined we get cynicism, which is a feature of self-knowing inverse hedonism.

In the first stanza Lowell describes his context and sets the scene. The scene is that of the journey; the context is

Reading how even the Swiss had thrown the sponge
in once again and Everest was still
unscaled

Lowell is probably referring to the Swiss expedition to Everest in
1952 which failed, but which prepared the way for Sir John
Hunt's successful British expedition later in the same year. The
metaphor appears to be in the renewed failure to reach the
heights of human aspiration, this time by the Swiss, who re-appear
later in the poem as Papal guards: the critical description here thus
serves a purpose later on. Lowell then introduces the personal
note already mentioned and allows an ambiguity to cover the
question of whether his reference is to St. Augustine's City of
God or to the physical city of Rome as residence of the Popes. In
other words, he leaves open the question of whether he is now
denying the essential truth of Catholic doctrine or whether he is
leaving Rome in disgust at the failure of the Church on earth to
live up to that doctrine. Essentially, the weight of the evidence
suggests an abandonment of the doctrine; but, in so far as myths
and religion embody aspiration rather than truth, Lowell continues to find them convenient points of reference for his attacks
on man. Some kind of standard, however skeletal, is still required
for judgement but, with this ambiguity, this refusal to commit
himself, Lowell denudes his standards of authority.

In the remaining lines of the first stanza, having expressed the
reluctance with which he departed from faith, Lowell introduces
a note of nostalgia, corroded with irony:

I envy the conspicuous
waste of our grandparents on their grand tours—
long-haired Victorian sages accepted the universe,
while breezing on their trust funds through the world.

The irony and contempt in these lines conveys the poet's claim to
superior insight to that of his ancestors: their sense of security, he
says, was false and (as described in his epithets) that makes them
ridiculous as well. Retrospectively this attack supports the criticism
of religion implicit in the earlier lines. Both the ambiguity and

the irony boost the claim to personal authority the poet makes in this stanza: but it is a corrupt claim, because only ambiguity and irony, not straightforward argument, support it.

In the second stanza Lowell moves from introductory notation to the substance of doctrine itself

> When the Vatican made Mary's Assumption dogma,

The rest of the stanza is, then, essentially a comment or judgement on the doctrine of the assumption—the doctrine defined by Pope Pius XII in 1950, stating that, on her death, the Virgin Mary was assumed, body and soul, into heaven. Lowell goes on

> the crowds at San Pietro screamed *Papa*.
> The Holy Father dropped his shaving glass,
> and listened. His electric razor purred,
> his pet canary chirped on his left hand.
> The lights of science couldn't hold a candle
> to Mary risen—at one miraculous stroke,
> angel-wing'd, gorgeous as a jungle bird!

The first line of this stanza established what has happened; the rest of the stanza depicts responses to the happening and responses to the responses. The second line is the response of the people who, in screaming for the Pope, identify him with the dogma and thus with the truth of God. The third, fourth and fifth lines describe the Pope's response to this phenomenon. The formula of description used, however, is deliberately alien, as a response, both to the emotion and the dogma. What purports to be a response is not a response at all. This tableau is followed by three crudely jocose lines; it is by no means clear whose comment these represent—the Pope's or the poet's. There are three possibilities: the lines may be the Pope's cynical comment; they may be the Pope's genuine comment, in which case their crudity is inadequate as a response; they may be the poet's comment. In any case, the ambiguity is so great, the possibilities and mixtures of them so various that one is forced to conclude that the poet is saying nothing and using a crude, vulgar and biased irony to conceal that fact.

The next line is apparently the most straightforward and unambiguous in the poem; it is in fact the most deeply ambiguous:

> But who believed this? Who could understand?

The line is followed by this passage:

> Pilgrims still kissed St. Peter's brazen sandal.
> The Duce's lynched, bare, booted skull still spoke.
> God herded his people to the *coup de grâce*—
> the costumed Switzers sloped their pikes to push,
> O Pius, through the monstrous human crush . . .

The first line quoted in this paragraph might be taken to mean that a (possibly true) doctrine was not appreciated by the mob (with the possible corollary implication that, if not appreciated it was not true, an interpretation encouraged by the various meanings possible in the Pope's response). If the emphasis is put on the first half of the line, however, an element of sanction is given to this belief; the meaning then is that people capable of intellectual effort (the poet) cannot understand the significance of the doctrine, while the crowds in line two cannot understand, in the sense of acting upon, its meaning. The verbosity of lines six to eight, compared to the ordinary humanity of lines two to five, support this interpretation. The rest of the stanza shows that, in any event, behaviour is not altered by the dogma—a crucial litmus-paper test of truth central to Lowell's doctrine in *Life Studies*. Now, if the last three lines of the stanza are taken to depend on the fourth last line, 'God' in the third last line might be taken for a savage and justifiable irony that is, one meaning that God *allows* this bestiality in his people. But the quatrain is preceded by

> Pilgrims still kissed St. Peter's brazen sandal.

'Still' here is crucial: it gives a critical overtone to the line (a line describing an ordinary and traditional act of reverence) and associates it with the following four lines. The activity of kissing

the sandal becomes associated, in the same line of thought following doubt and disbelief, with the Duce, the herding of the people,
the callous crowd control of the Swiss guards and the association
of the Pope with a 'monstrous' human crush, suggesting an
offence against Pius's sense of delicacy.

Yet the activities in these lines are not comparable unless made
so by the poet. The process of making them comparable is not
one of argument but of juxtaposition; and that is not even juxtaposition of obviously valid or objective concepts, but of particular
forms of words, selected by the poet, and being no necessary
relevance to reality or truth. If we trace the argument back from
the end of the second stanza, through its ambiguities and crude
ironies, we will find that, ultimately, it depends on

> Much against my will,
> I left the City of God where it belongs.

The last three words of the second line, with their dismissive overtone, deserve emphasis: what Lowell is saying in the second
stanza is that all of the argument is true because he says it is. Given
this fundamental position, the exact character, meaning or quality
of the argument, poetic or rational, in the second stanza, has no
relevance: it need be neither true nor pointed, neither witty nor
plausible. The poet may select what he likes, to prove what he
likes and he is not even obliged to give a meaning to the second
stanza because that, too, is irrelevant. What matters is not
whether justification for despair or abandonment of belief exist,
but whether the poet feels they do or not. In a profound sense the
second stanza is meaningless and nihilistic: it is inverse hedonism
at its very worst.

It is depressing to go on. Even as it is, I have only touched on
the ambiguities and evasions of the opening stanzas; but, however pursued, these come to the conclusion outlined above. Nor is
there any rescue of the poem in the third and fourth stanzas. In
the third stanza Ovid is set off against Lucan, Tacitus and Juvenal
who, in the ambiguity of the stanza could be represented as poets
serving or poets destroying the brutalised Roman Empire. This

potentially fruitfully ambiguous account of the role of poetry must, however, be set off against the final Ovidian statement:

> 'Imperial Tiber, Oh my yellow dog,
> black earth by the black Roman sea, I lie
> with the boy-crazy daughter of the God,
> *Il duce Augusto*. I shall never die.'

The Rome of the Caesars is tied to that of Mussolini in *Il duce Augusto*; Ovid is critical of Imperial Rome as Lowell is of modern Papal Rome; a hint that he is more than 'pure prose' is suggested in the last line, but this is no more than, like the references in the first stanza, an unfulfilled hint, bought at the sacrifice of involving Ovid in the personalised doctrines of the first and second stanzas.

In the last stanza the theme of aspiration, conceived in terms of altitude, but of aspiration failed and frustrated, is renewed. Minerva

> prince, pope, philosopher and golden bough

is that aspiration but

> each backward, wasted Alp a Parthenon,
> fire-branded socket of the Cyclop's eye

—the cult of Minerva is in ruins. And, in any event, that cult may have been itself ruinous

> pure mind and murder at the scything prow—
> Minerva, the miscarriage of the brain.

What this couplet suggests is the most despairing of all points in the poem: the mind, which can perceive all aspiration (and write poetry) is a 'miscarriage'. I cannot, therefore, see this poem as Mr. Staples does, as a noble grappling with human limitations. Even the famous last Imagist couplet

> Now Paris, our black classic, breaking up
> like killer kings on an Etruscan cup.

though magniloquent, means nothing but nihilism when the rest of the argument of the poem is taken into account.

Yet the ambiguities, the points where Lowell does not quite commit himself to the implications of his poem, persist in the mind: alas, they add titillation to hedonistic obscurity as characteristics of 'Beyond the Alps'. I have analysed that poem at great length for reasons that will become apparent, reasons two among which may be mentioned now: its length and range make it a revealing panorama of preoccupations and techniques; and its tendencies dominate or greatly influence *Life Studies* up to, but excluding, the last poem, 'Skunk Hour'.

There is also here a lesson for literary critics and particularly for critics of Lowell. In my view this is a 'bad' poem, but by that I do not mean an incompetent poem. It is a poem of considerable, but misused, talent, of talent bent on evasion rather than statement. Here is the lesson, for we do tend to equate badness with incompetence and though this is sometimes true it is by no means always the case. A casual reader, for example, might well be puzzled by what might seem to be my arbitrary inclination to praise or damn Lowell's work extravagantly. There is no contradiction, except between occasions on which he uses his talent well and occasions on which he uses it ill. The talent is a constant; the poet's moral stability is not. And in the criticism of poetry we must re-learn the basic rules of judgement: lack of talent is not the only equation with badness. Indeed, the real attacking purpose of criticism is not against incompetence (though it may be against fashion) but against the misuse of ability and the propagation of false and corrupting poetic doctrines.

More is at issue here than the reputation of a simple poet, however distinguished. I have suggested that ambiguity, obscurity, evasion and irony—however it is put, lack of straightforwardness—are all techniques employed to a bad end in 'Beyond the Alps'. We may fail to detect this because in such training as we have received in the modern schools of literary criticism, obscurity, difficulty of elucidation, is too often taken as a sign of achievement. It may be—more often than not, when a talented critic is attracted to it, it is—a sign of *talent*, but not achievement. That equation between ambiguity and success must go.

This is a matter of the greatest importance. As the poet is in search of the expression of just feeling, so the critic is in search of just appreciation. We get merely a double corruption if the poet's purpose is *simply* to express intense or *purely* personal feeling and if the critic is out merely to explain and justify his own reaction to the text. We get, indeed, merely a double repetition of the hedonistic heresy that insight is superior to argument. We ought to know that insight—the act of apprehension of experience— exists for purposes of communication only if it is transmitted with emotional force, sustained by argument. The quality of the argument reveals the quality of the insight.

'Beyond the Alps' is, in many ways, a beguiling example of Lowell's craft, as many of his bad poems are. Its resonances are multiple and its ambiguities manifold. One is justified, I believe, in saying that neither its feelings nor its judgements are justly or properly (that is, morally) motivated. Further, one can say that the overlap of different kinds of image and situation, without a strong thread of meaning but with, rather, a strong thread of mood running through them, may conceal the reference back of the poem to the poet's unadulterated personality as a source of authority and to his basic conviction—the sameness through time of the corruption of man, itself a corruption of his insight into the contemporaneity of history.

But it would be foolish to imagine that Lowell goes out of his way to clarify the situation for us, that he makes unequivocally clear where he believes the source of his authority to lie. The equivocation as to source is, of course, an uncertainty as to the meaning—the moral progression—of the poem, for it cannot be claimed that this series of ambiguities contributes to the argument in any way. The ambiguities, then, serve not to enlarge experience but to conceal the poet.

An elucidation of William Empson's theory of ambiguities would not, I think, help here. But Empson did distinguish between good (that is, effective) ambiguity and bad (that is, ineffective) ambiguity. I would like to call these positive and negative. Negative ambiguity is what we have been discussing in Lowell. It may represent one of three things. It may represent an inner uncertainty on the poet's part, which may take the form of genuine doubt, which in his professional character he tries to conceal rather than express; it may be self indulgence, that is, Lowell may actually believe that this tortuous mode of expression, proceeding from his personality, is true, just and properly motivated feeling; or it may represent an intermittent functioning of sensibility, in which Lowell is variable in his taste and judgement. In an obvious way this is suggested by the last word of the following extract from 'Inauguration Day 1953', the third poem in *Life Studies*:

> Cyclonic zero of the Word,
> God of our armies, who interred
> Cold Harbor's blue immortals, Grant!
> Horseman, your sword is in the groove!

The last word fails for a number of reasons, but principally because it is inadequate to sustain the linguistic force of Lowell's earlier pronouncements or to transmit that force to the final quatrain:

> Look, the fixed stars, all just alike
> as lack-land atoms, split apart,
> and the Republic summons Ike,
> the mausoleum in her heart.

This is not a very striking poem, but it serves the purpose of illustration very well. Roughly, Lowell is saying that General Eisenhower is an inadequate President for the present crisis and by extension to Grant, that generals make bad Presidents. One line conveys wonderfully well his sense of the urgency of the crisis and the precise, stagnant character of the present situation (the metaphor in this poem is also that of a journey):

> Ice, ice. Our wheels no longer move;

Now, in my submission, 'mausoleum' potentially rescues the

poem from 'groove', which is crude and tasteless. That is because of the resonance of the word, its associations of grandeur. It is used bitterly, almost in disgust, but not without a sense of reverberation, an awareness of the strength of the opposition. 'Groove', on the other hand, is used contemptuously in a minor key: the feeling it evokes is inappropriate to the crisis as well as to the feeling with which the poet evokes that crisis. 'Mausoleum', has, I believe, positive ambiguity to some extent: one possible meaning to draw from it is its hint of a grand monument to a distinguished past, which conveys the concomitant suggestion that Lowell has selected between strength (even if used to a bad purpose) and weakness in his opposition.

'Inauguration Day', then, conveys a positive note. That note is rarely wholly absent from Lowell and, for reasons which will become clear as I go along, I believe that 'Beyond the Alps' is not altogether without encouragement either for, in my opinion, the concealment of precisely what he is about there demonstrates a fruitful uncertainty on Lowell's part. In other words, his critical intellect feels doubt about his method of proceeding: his difficulty arises from his sense—his deepest instinct—that the impulses of his personality are a surer ultimate guide to truth than his intelligence. To a very great extent, but not wholly with success, that difficulty was resolved (temporarily at least) in 'Skunk Hour', but not until then.

The stress I have laid on negative ambiguity helps to highlight another important characteristic, both of Lowell's intention in this volume and of the actually completed work. I have tried to show the nature, purpose and effect of negative ambiguity in 'Beyond the Alps': essentially, it concealed indecision and the inability of the poet to discover material on which decision could be based. But Lowell was not truly happy with the experiment of resorting to his own personality: the drive behind the change of direction in *Life Studies* is to be seen in a passage from the prose essay '91 Revere Street' (Part II of the American *Life Studies*, omitted in the first English edition but included in the second). In the house, Lowell writes

'. . . the vast number of remembered *things* remains rocklike. Each is in its place, each has its function, its history, its drama. There, all is preserved by the motherly care that one either ignored or resented in his youth. The things and their owners come back urgent with life and meaning—because finished, they are endurable and perfect.'

Eleven of the fifteen life studies in Part IV of the volume have, then, the purpose of fixing experience and rendering it imperishable and so objective. I want to look first at the longest poem (which opens the sequence), 'My last afternoon with Uncle Devereux Winslow'. This poem is calm, in tone, almost resigned; Lowell seems to be searching for meaning as much as he asserts it. The advice which dominates is that of the adult poet looking at the child's experience of life through the child's eyes and thus assessing, not only the child, but what the child sees (a method used with some effect in 'The First Sunday in Lent'). This device is decorated by a careful pattern of imagery, based on the elements earth, air and water.

The date of the events in the poem is 1922; Lowell is five and a half years old. In the four stanzas of Part I he sets the place (his grandfather's summer house) and the mood, one of calm, slightly disturbed by a child's fractiousness. The second stanza introduces the important image of the child playing with black earth and lime, both symbols of death, likely to coagulate, with a corpse into one substance. The stanza goes on to identify the décor with the poet's grandfather, 'manly, comfortable/overbearing, disproportioned'. The third extends this description of the place and its people, identifying the one with the other, but contrasting, nonetheless, the validity of the material with the *bric-à-brac* mutability of the people and their activities and stressing, behind all, the susceptibility of place as well as people to alteration, change and decay.

Part II consists of one short stanza in which the child dressed in his 'formal pearl grey shorts' sees himself first as an 'Olympian' figure as impressive and perfect as his solid, material toys before he realises, seeing his wet face distorted in 'the basin's mirror', not as what he thought he was but as 'a stuffed toucan/with a bibulous, multi-colored beak'. The child is thus identified with the process outlined in Part I: he does not understand this experience, the meaning of which is explained for him in the stanza by the adult poet.

Part III describes, in two stanzas, Lowell's great-aunt Sarah; her best days, in which she 'jilted an Astor' are gone, and she sits upstairs playing a dummy piano, bought to soothe the ears of Grandmother, engaged, that is, on a purposeless, dead activity. The element 'air' is introduced in a double meaning sense in this stanza, unsuccessfully, in my opinion.

Part IV consists of three stanzas. The first is mere description, serving to introduce Uncle Devereux. The second fixes Devereux against the background of his possessions and surroundings. The third tells him abruptly that

> My Uncle was dying at twenty-nine.

In the light of this shocking evidence of mortality the whole scene is reviewed again. Devereux Winslow is further identified with the material background, now considered for its more ludicrous and inanimate characteristics. The approaching mood of elevated adult apprehension of death is introduced by a classical comparison of the child to Agrippina and the poem ends by underlining the significance of the earth and lime image:

> My hands were warm, then cool, on the piles
> of earth and lime,
> A black pile and a white pile . . .
> Come winter,
> Uncle Devereux would blend to the one colour.

This is an ambitious and elaborate poem, but I do not find it at all a successful one. It is another approach by Lowell to the problem of chronicling decay and mutability, finding the material that will strengthen his statement and appropriately introducing his own personality. Although the imagery is elaborate, the construction of the argument and the syntax of the poem are themselves very loose and random. There is no discrimination or appropriateness, no force of judgement in the material.

Yet this poem has been widely praised. Because I find its construction loose and arbitrary an analysis showing in detail what I found wrong with it would be grossly and tediously extended. I will therefore confine my points to the few I consider really substantial, erect a generalisation out of those and illustrate my meaning with a comparison.

I said earlier that the method of 'Beyond the Alps' concealed Lowell's moral indecision. A facet of this phenomenon was the arbitrariness with which elements of his subjects were selected: because arbitrary, their significance was unclear. In this poem the selection is equally arbitrary: there is no particular or traditional significance in the local images (that is, those pertaining to the family's possessions and surroundings) put on parade. What significance they eventually possess is given them by the adjectival insertions of the poet—'Diamond-pointed poplars', 'bibulous' beaks etc.—building up into the earth, water, air sequence of imagery. The pattern is strengthened by the overall imagistic sequence, but the whole rests on the convention of the adult seeing through the child's eyes—a convention which Mr. Staples (who admires the poem) regards as essential to its success.

I have nothing against the use of the convention as such: indeed, the reader may remember that I praised a similar usage in Wordsworth. With Lucy, however, elaboration of the implications of the convention took place within a brief and tightly constructed argument. In this poem the convention permits Lowell the child to perform the business of the arbitrary selection of materials which are then adjectivally invested with significance. Ultimately, again, significance depends on the whim of the poet's personality, decorated by his talent—and the personality, indeed, at a naive and impressionable age, such being the convention. The whole sustains a very simple thesis—not only the immutability and decay of everything but, worse, the *equal* and immutable decay of everything. In this scheme of things all experiences are equal in value and impact and therefore in significance. This is a destructive doctrine.

I would like to illustrate these general remarks and meet an objection at the same time. The third stanza of Part IV opens in this way:

> My uncle was dying at twenty-nine
> 'You are behaving like children,'
> Said my Grandfather,
> When my Uncle and Aunt left their three baby daughters
> and sailed for Europe on a last honeymoon . . .
> I cowered in terror.
> I wasn't a child at all—
> Unseen and all-seeing, I was Agrippina
> in the Golden House of Nero . . .

The first line is, as Mr. Staples says, the 'revelation' of the poem: he finds it 'as shocking in its suddenness as E. M. Forster's famous "Gerald died that afternoon." ' The comparison illuminates my point. Without going into the merits and demerits of Forster's novel it may be said that the reason we find the death shocking is our absorption up to that point in the careful way in which the author built up Gerald as a powerful physical life force, contrasted to the flickering flame of Rickie. The suddenness of his death affects us because of the terrible implication of Fate and Mortality it carries. The effect is also ironic, in that Ricky then marries Gerald's girl who was essentially attracted to Gerald by his animal vivacity. Other ironies follow in a rich pattern, illustrating the tragic situation of a man of ability deprived by some inner fault of the ability to assert himself against circumstances. Lowell's revelation is merely abrupt, because the preceding pattern of preparation is arbitrary and whimsical. Forster forces us to look back and enrich our shock by all that has gone before.

There are numerous local ironies in the next three lines and some conventional sadness in the fourth. But these deliberately break what impact the first line has and interrupt the progression to the Agrippina lines, while the local irony (the play upon 'children') detracts from the strength of the structure as a whole. In the sixth, seventh, eighth and ninth lines, however, a deliberate portentousness and sense of significance enters, the meaning of

which is quite unclear. Is it child or poet who sees the meaning of
the previous lines? Is it, perhaps, that the child senses and the poet
sees? What is the meaning of the historical comparison? No
forceful or poetic guide to elucidation is given: we have
portentousness without point.

There is, here, a general problem as well as one peculiar to
Lowell. I hope to illustrate its nature by a sidelight. I suggested
earlier that one could sense a dissatisfaction with his work in
Lowell, produced by a clash between the impulses of his personality and his critical intellect. The problem is that his personality is dominated by a rather vague sense of catastrophe, ruin,
deceit and decay: it is subject to no discipline outside itself. Now,
I also hinted at my belief that, nonetheless, the personality rather
than the intellect was Lowell's true guide. Now, what he wants to
render—the form his instinctive judgement takes—is that of
a chaotic and dissolved state of emotion: the problem is, if
the state of emotion is significant, to place it in a context
where its significance will be apparent and to construct such a
context.

In one view, that establishment of context is a technical
problem. But it depends on two quite different things which we
must be quite clear about in our minds though, in practice, in the
text, they are indissolubly linked. The first of these is an ordered
system of moral value, the effect of the decline of which I tried to
explain in my first chapter. A system of value, to adumbrate,
invests gesture and action with significance. In its turn it depends
on an impulse of moral knowledge which is scrutinised and made
into form—made into a rational code of behaviour—by the intelligence. The code depends on the impulse but the impulse is given
meaning by the code: thus are both made both beautiful and true,
by their interaction with one another. When we read great poetry
our reaction to it is one initially of instinct, it is a reaction of
sensibility, which combines intellect and feeling. Now, our subsequent scrutiny of the poem cannot be merely a justification of
that instinct: that practice, as I said earlier, is corrupt and un-
reasonable. Rather, we examine, with our sensibility the structure
of the poem—the evidence it offers of the poet's awareness of a

system of moral value, judgement and discrimination. Through that scrutiny we uncover the initial moral impulse, which makes its appearance in the system. The impulse is, hypothetically, prior to the system, but it cannot be manifest except *in* the system. The continued existence of a system, even if it is corrupt or decadent in some way, implies the continued existence of the impulse. The detection and scrutiny of either one, however, made difficult by the intrusion of the poet's personality, which tends to make the system individualistic and, hence, alien. To some degree, after the intrusion of the personality, the original impulse and the personality are in intimate relation to one another. Hypothetically, this is no bad thing—indeed, it could be an enrichment—but experience suggests that the impact of the personality will be to a degree destructive of any existing system. To some extent the poet will have to modify or remake the system he finds. *Poems 1938–49* was a modification; *Life Studies* is a re-making—so far as my scrutiny has gone, one I have found unsuccessful, because the system created is arbitrary and whimsical. But I think it is clear enough what Lowell is trying to do, and his attempt supports the general line of reasoning in these remarks. Some system is required for the establishment of the necessary context.

But there is a second aspect of the problem that, for a moment, I may be permitted to regard as purely technical. (I put it this way merely to illustrate: technical separation of one aspect of literature is like a laboratory experiment, divorced from human, that is, moral, reality.) That is the aspect of form. In poetry form is not merely metre, though metre is a part of form unique to poetry. To speak truly, form lies in the arrangement of the syntax of a piece of literature. It can lie partly in imagery and Lowell tried to make it nearly wholly do so in 'My Last Afternoon'. That was not, however, a success, a general reason for which I will suggest later on. For the moment, however, I merely wish to stress the significant part technique in the use of language may play in the establishment of a poetic context.

In the third last paragraph I tried to describe the state of emotion with which Lowell starts his work. I now want to quote a passage from Jane Austen where the author describes a similar state of dissolution of spirit. It is from *Persuasion*: Walter, Anne's nephew, hangs from her neck and she cannot shake him off:

> 'But not a bit did Walter stir.
>
> In another moment, however, she found herself in the state of being released from him: someone was taking him from her, though he had bent down her head so much that his little sturdy hands were unfastened from around her neck, and he was resolutely borne away, before she knew that Captain Wentworth had done it.
>
> Her sensations on the discovery made her perfectly speechless. She could not even thank him. She could only hang over little Charles, with most disordered feelings. His kindness in stepping forward to her relief, the manner, the silence in which it had passed, the little particulars of the circumstance, with the conviction soon forced upon her, by the noise he was studiously making with the child, that he meant to avoid hearing her thanks, and rather sought to testify that her conversation was the last of his wants, produced such a confusion of varying but very painful agitation as she could not recover from, till enabled, by the entrance of Mary and the Miss Musgroves, to make over her little patient to their cares, and leave the room.'

Here is an incident, paltry in itself, invested with great significance. The whole of this chapter would be needed to do justice to its truth and beauty. Our appreciation of this increases, of course, when we know that this is the full re-awakening of Anne's love for Wentworth. The full effect of the disorder of feeling of which the author speaks can only be grasped within the total context of the novels, concerned as they are to a great degree with moral control of behaviour. Nonetheless, the passage can stand alone. When we look at it alone we can see the tremendous range of understanding Jane Austen encompasses. The contrast in the passage is between the insignificance of each detail of what happens and the trauma Anne is going through: as the full scale of the trauma becomes apparent the details noted become more insignificant, the gestures of the socially conventional setting more stark and ritualised. The very insignificance of what happens, in a word, increases the significance of what happens and that is a manifestation of the writer's astonishing range and control. The fourth sentence of the third paragraph shows that control at full power, reflecting the state of Anne's mind and noting even more precisely what is happening. But the long slow movement of the first sentence of the second paragraph—with the pregnant word 'state'— should also be noted for the way in which the ground is prepared. Yet the whole passage is one in which significance is concealed and even, by convention, belied: it is a great passage of positive ambiguity.

I chose this passage because it is a remarkable example of an occasion on which technique and moral sensibility, though working side by side, can almost be seen separately. That is, comparatively, a fault: in a similar, but much more powerful scene—the one in *Emma* in which Knightley and Emma discover their love for one another—the two things cannot so readily be seen, and the passage represents a greater synthesis.

Of course, it could be denied that this passage in *Persuasion* offers a true comparison with Lowell in that the feeling of love Jane Austen describes is positive while the feeling of ruin possessing Lowell is negative. The objection has force, but I feel the analogy is made valid by the similarity of the intention of detecting meaning in trivia. I believe that the Jane Austen passages show more effectively than I could in argument the essential truth of the theory of poetry I have been offering in criticism of some of Lowell's practice: the order on which art depends is an essentially moral and formal order which, and the command over which, demonstrates the objective value and quality of the artist's initial impulse.

Earlier in this chapter I quoted a comment by Mr. Hamilton on the comparison between a passage of Lowell's prose and a passage of verse from another of the *Life Studies*, 'Commander Lowell'. The dissolution of formal control in Lowell shown by that comparison suggests to me that dissolved feeling itself dissolves form. So uncertain and generalised a feeling as is exhibited throughout much of *Life Studies* is necessarily reflected in the lax syntactical organisation of the work. Discipline most often exists in image patterns but these are injections of significance after thought, rather than a true synthesis.

There is, however, a distinctly human note of affection in the life studies themselves which, though they exhibit most of the faults of 'My last afternoon' does provide a certain appeal. 'Dunbarton' and 'Grandparents' record that lax, gentle affection:

> In the mornings I cuddled like a paramour
> in my Grandfather's bed
> While he scouted about the chattering greenwood stove.

But Lowell can quickly destroy this mood with an injection of significance:

> My Grandfather found
> his grandchild's fogbound solitudes
> sweeter than human society.

In 'Terminal Days at Beverly Farm', however, the sad, final note accompanying his father's illness and death is added to with a waspish note:

> He smiled his oval Lowell smile,
> he wore his cream gabardine dinner jacket,
> and indigo cummerbund.

None of these life studies merit much analysis; there is little more in them after 'My last afternoon' than biographical interest. The worst of the sheer chronicling of objects with no very clear purpose is in 'During Fever':

> Mother, your master bedroom
> looked away from the ocean.
> You had a window-seat,
> an electric blanket,
> a silver hot water bottle
> monogrammed like a hip-flask,
> Italian china fruity
> with bunches and berries
> and proper *putti*.

There is little that is much better except 'For Sale', a short poem
noting in a sad, limited but sharply effective way his mother's
reaction to his father's death and events following: his father's
cottage is

> Empty, open, intimate,
> its town-house furniture
> had an on tiptoe air
> of waiting for the mover
> on the heels of the undertaker.
> Ready, afraid
> of living alone till eighty,
> Mother mooned in a window,
> as if she had stayed on a train
> one stop past her destination.

On the whole, then, these small, limited poems are the result of
the doctrine of the significance of the object outlined in the passage quoted earlier from '91 Revere Street' which was itself
derived from the doctrines of personality and dissolution of
sensibility and discrimination chronicled in these pages and common to contemporaries as well as Lowell. The earlier poems in
the volume have little to offer: four poems 'On Ford Madox
Ford', 'George Santayana', 'Delmore Schwartz' and 'Hart Crane'
reflect the characters of their subjects well and exhibit Lowell's
unease. But they are important only in his evolution and can be
noted later. 'The Bank's Daughter' is an unclear mixture of the
colloquial and the pretentious and 'A Mad Negro Soldier confined at Munich' is vulgar and undisciplined. If the poems examined
up to now were all Lowell offered in *Life Studies* the disappoint-
ment would have been great.

But there is something more. To take them in order 'Waking
in the Blue' tells of Lowell's time in a mental home; 'Home after
three months away' chronicles his return; 'Memories of West
Street and Lepke' I have already discussed; 'Man and Wife' discusses the relationship of a mentally disturbed man (Lowell himself) and his wife; ' "To speak of the love that is in marriage" '
contains general reflections on marriage of a manic character in a

fine, disciplined form and 'Skunk Hour' is a final, astonishing appreciation of madness, ruin and all the disintegrating pre-occupations of Lowell's career to date.

The achievement in these poems is far from even, but they show a remarkable capacity for self-appraisal and a remarkable ability to venture out again, to continue the unrelenting search for resources. 'Waking in the Blue', though it is not a particularly good poem and much of its detail is incidental, possesses a tone of horrified irony at the situation of an intelligent and gifted man in an asylum—and notes precisely the sordidity, moral as well as physical, of the surroundings. Lowell objectifies his plight very successfully, with a certain grim humour:

> (This is the house for the 'mentally ill'.)

> What use is my sense of humour?
> I grin at 'Stanley', now sunk in his sixties,
> once a Harvard all-American fullback,

And, at the end, Lowell distinguishes between himself and his fellow-patients in an effective way that heightens the horror in his final identification with them:

> After a hearty New England breakfast,
> I weigh two hundred pounds
> this morning. Cock of the walk,
> I strut in my turtle-necked French sailor's jersey
> before the metal shaving mirrors,
> and see the shaky future grow familiar
> in the pinched, indigenous faces
> of these thoroughbred mental cases,
> twice my age and half my weight.
> We are all old timers,
> each of us holds a locked razor.

The sudden shift of rhythm and pattern in the last line is what gives this stanza its remarkable effectiveness. More important, however, is how Lowell is able to truly invest detail with significance in the moral context he is constructing for himself. His own penchant for rather hearty crudity of expression is put to good use in the first four lines and the precision of 'metal' (not glass for fear of suicide) in the next line shivers with meaning. There is a decent, human charity for his less well-fed fellows, a direct sympathy rarely seen before, in the following lines before the final grim note is struck.

This is the first poem scrutinised in this chapter, or in any chapter since the introduction, in which, with Lowell, we feel the direct transmission of a lived experience. It is not (none of these terminal life studies are) possessed of the range and universality of 'The Holy Innocents' or 'Mr. Edwards and the Spider' but it is direct, precise and genuine. Possessing feeling, it is not emotional because Lowell's cool intellect reacts so appropriately—so courageously—to his experience. The fact that we never doubt his mental disturbance is a tribute as much to his own informed acceptance of his condition as it is to the harsh jumble of the first stanza, in which the scene is set. Here, then, out of personality and experience, Lowell has built a true structure, at least in the final stanza, as some of the earlier ones are flawed.

'Home after three months away' has the sad note with which we are becoming familiar. Two things about it are worth notice. The first is the continuance of the gentle strain of human intimacy so successfully conveyed in the precise placing of 'Dearest' in the following passage about his daughter:

> After thirteen weeks
> my child still dabs her cheeks
> to start me shaving. When
> we dress her in her sky-blue corduroy,
> she changes to a boy,
> and floats my shaving brush
> and washcloth in the flush . . .
> Dearest, I cannot loiter here
> in lather like a polar bear.

But this passage relates directly to the last stanza of the previous poem. Lowell can now be trusted with a razor again. This enables

him to return to human society. That return, however, involves
more than the enjoyment of that society, even in the appealing
guise of his daughter. He notes, in the next stanza, that 'Recuperat-
ing, I neither spin nor toil' and directly questions and tests the
resources he now possesses: has he lost something in the cure?

> I keep no rank nor station
> Cured, I am frizzled, stale and small.

This is the end of a cycle and here the authoritative personality of
'Beyond the Alps' is subjected to remorseless scrutiny. The burden
must, however, be shouldered again and it is therefore significant
that, after these two essentially stabilising, direct poems, Lowell
places the final four poems that explore the nature, importance
and consequences of his madness. The couplet quoted above
finally relates, as I hope to show, to the sixth stanza of 'Skunk
Hour'.

'West Street and Lepke' tests Lowell's renewed energies as a
public poet. I believe, for reasons stated earlier, that it is a failure
and a regression. 'Man and Wife' is less so. Its picture of the comfort his wife gave at great personal cost, during his illness, is
beautifully conveyed:

> All night I've held your hand,
> as if you had
> a fourth time faced the kingdom of the mad—
> its hackneyed speech, its homicidal eye—
> and dragged me home alive.

Lowell's assurance and control here are impressive. It fades rather
into shrillness in describing their earlier relationship and the
exhaustion of his wife, now alienated as a consequence of her
struggle: it ends in a passage not remotely as direct or controlled
as the one above, indeed, in another forceful, but not pointed,
image:

> Now twelve years later, you turn your back.
> Sleepless, you hold

your pillow to your hollows like a child,
your old-fashioned tirade—
loving, rapid, merciless—
breaks like the Atlantic Ocean on my head.

Judgement and meaning are here again uncertain. But, in the next poem, Lowell looks at a situation of this kind from the wife's point of view and paints a truly terrifying picture of her fear set against madness in lines of racing power and graphic imagery:

My hopped up husband drops his home disputes,
and hits the streets to cruise for prostitutes,
free-lancing out along the razor's edge.
This screwball might kill his wife, then take the pledge.
Oh the monotonous meanness of his lust.

The crudeness of the domestic imagery is effectively contrasted here to the sharp anarchy of the description of the husband's extra-moral activity. The whole poem has mixed into it a manic fascination with the condition on the poet's part and this gives it an extra dimension. There is a quite remarkable concentration and focus of energy here, but not a great deal of range. Control is maintained by keeping to a short description of madness a condition, in the virulent form described here, not admitting of much enlargement and explanation of a firm kind. In danger of writing a mad poem, Lowell contrives to write a poem about madness. The achievement is distinct; personally it may well have been heroic; objectively and poetically it is limited. This is shown in the return of the last four lines first to the crude, domestic imagery and then to another concentrated but limited and narrow description of the horror of the wife's experience of her husband's condition:

What makes him tick? Each night now I tie
ten dollars and his car key to my thigh . . .
Gored by the climacteric of his want,
he stalls above me like an elephant.

These poems can be seen as a preparation for 'Skunk Hour'. In that poem Lowell faces more directly than ever before the two main problems of this phase of his career, the quality of his personality as a source of judgement and the insight that sees equal dissolution in everything and cannot discriminate between evidence, being forced to render everything with equal emphasis. I have already spoken of the character and merits of this poem to some extent in Chapter One and I want here to concentrate principally on elements assisting in the development of the theme of this chapter.

'Skunk Hour' consists of eight short stanzas describing, apparently, the neighbourhood around Lowell's summer home. The phraseology is short, flat and declarative, each stanza being a variation on its predecessor. The subject is, again, the decline and decadence of New England. The first stanza reads

> Nautilus Island's hermit
> heiress still lives through winter in her Spartan cottage;
> her sheep still graze above the sea.
> Her son's a bishop. Her farmer
> is first selectman in our village,
> she's in her dotage.

This simple description is elaborated in the next stanza. The dotage is seen to be destructive as the heiress buys up 'the eyesores' 'and lets them fall'. It establishes, however, the power of money as an integral and controlling feature of the physical and social landscapes now connected with one another. In the next stanza, the connection is modified in the first line, which opens up a context again for the money theme (even this resource, the poet says, is gone) which in turn opens the way for a re-statement of the theme of the ruined landscape:

> The season's ill—
> we've lost our summer millionaire,
> . . .
> A red fox stain covers Blue Hill.

Here the perception wavers. A decorator is introduced who unsuccessfully potters at brightening up his own surroundings before the poet himself moves into the landscape. He instantly perceives its corruption of it but suddenly, in the last line, questions his capacity:

> One dark night,
> my Tudor Ford climbed the hill's skull,
> I watched for love-cars. Lights turned down,
> they lay together, hull to hull,
> where the graveyard shelves on the town . . .
> My mind's not right.

In other words, in watching for love-cars Lowell recognises a morbid propensity on his part: he seeks out corruption and ruin and this instinct suggests a doubtful judgement. In the next stanza he faces the full implication of this realisation:

> A car radio bleats,
> 'Love, O careless Love . . .' I hear
> my ill-spirit sob in each blood cell,
> as if my hand were at its throat . . .
> I myself am hell,
> nobody's here—

It would be ungenerous not to salute the singular personal courage of this stanza while recognising its remarkable personal achievement. If 'nobody's here' Lowell's entire life's work has been merely a minute and morbid persecution of himself, with none of the objectivity and resource so stubbornly fought for. This possibility is seen, faced and responded to in a brave question thrown by himself at the integrity, character and value of himself, without influences or interruptions from outside. Moreover, the personality, the personal commitment to discovery and truth without question adds remarkable force to the lines: here, as Yeats might say, a man's passionate personality, unflawed by indulgence or whim, has given force to his utterance.

From this pinnacle Lowell explores, in the remaining two

stanzas, the skunk image which he then abruptly introduces. I have already commented (p. 20) on the final stanza. I want here merely to note that it is open to us to re-identify the skunk with man but that, in the final stanza Lowell personally assumes the burden of elaboration, as in the sixth stanza he assumes the burden of statement. His authority is established, and it lies in himself.

Lowell afterwards said that he was uncertain whether *Life Studies* was a death-rope or a lifeline. In the final analysis that does summarise the state of precarious equilibrium in which he is left at the end of the volume. For, as after 'The Holy Innocents' and 'Mr. Edwards and the Spider' one feels that the resources presented are strictly limited; the material they offer for extrapolation into future poetry seems distinctly thin and Lowell could not, clearly, simply go on staring madness in the face. The great hope for *Life Studies* was, however, that he had cleansed and purified his personality as an instrument of judgement, and might re-assume more directly his public role, labouring, no doubt under the general difficulties of the personality as an instrument of judgement, but with his own personality now less flawed, less chaotic, more integrated, more coherent.

For the Union Dead is a volume of different moods and atmospheres, of controlled success and minor notation. But it is, not only implicitly, but deliberately and obviously, heir to the purgation of *Life Studies*. For the first time Lowell encompasses all of his historical and individual themes in one body and attempts rationally to discriminate between, and to weigh and assess, experience. Several of the thirty-five poems actually pick up and re-examine themes and episodes of the earlier work in the light of his new equilibrium and control.

I want to make it clear at the outset that Lowell seems to me to achieve his long-sought-for balance of judgement and resources in this volume. In it, too, he returns almost aggressively to his open vocation as a public poet: the motto of the title poem is 'Relinquunt Omnia Servare Rem Publicam'. In this poem, and generally in the volume, he re-discovers the contemporaneity of history, but this time it is used in a positive sense, in that the past is encouraged to bring forward, not its sins only, but its virtues. The poet is personally involved in perceiving the distinction between the virtues and the vices of the past and in persecuting both. His diagnosis of the present, however, remains—and is reinforced as—a diagnosis of ruin. In that ruin, ambition as well as joy—ambition, that is, conceived as aspiration, as the will to abstract good through whatever action not distinctly evil—has departed. Consequently it is the sharply delineated and delimited aspirations of the past, as expressed in actions and monuments, that Lowell brings forward as judgements upon the present.

The refinement of the aspirations of the past, which is carried out painstakingly in the details of language, is directed towards establishing the existence of a purified moral strain. Now, that strain exists only in the poet and his poetry; Lowell is chronicling the public death of the generating moral impulse that I discussed in the last chapter and proving both its truth and its weight by seeking to define and articulate it by an appropriate artistic response to experience on his own part. The poems are now truly arguments of great cultural and moral significance: he does not always succeed in the personal act which discrimination is, but the direction of his effort is always clear. It is untainted by whim or self-indulgence and rarely flawed by the tendency to take appearance for reality or by the desire to censure indiscriminately.

Lowell offers his perceptions, such as they are, openly in this volume. By considering his own life as one of evolution, development and change, he offers the objectivity of his arguments for free and open inspection. His personality is as much the synthesising element as it was in the first phase of his career, but now the synthesis is created out of moral feeling rather than apocalyptic instinct. Given, then, the situation in which the personality of the poet is, in literature, a vital cement, and, to a degree, an independent source of insight, Lowell has tried to subject his personality to the same rigorous, discriminating scrutiny as he subjects his other material.

All of Lowell's work—with a few minor and aberrant exceptions—presumes the existence of absolute value. All good poetry must do this: where it appears not to we find that the poet takes very seriously the business of investigating the potential existence of absolute value so that, often paradoxically, the poem becomes a quest for that value. At each stage of Lowell's career there is a restatement, whether by way of repulsion or absorption, of the earlier stages, the earlier quest. In successive chapters I have tried, not only to describe his journey, but also to say where he was going and how far he had travelled. Only in my first chapter did I anticipate or range widely, trying rather to see each stage in and for itself and in the light of other stages. In *For the Union Dead* Lowell engages in the kind of retrospect the critic is himself obliged to undertake. From the vantage point of this volume, therefore, one can see more clearly than ever before how Lowell's preoccupations—often theoretically objective preoccupations—like religion—came, except at rare moments, between himself and just judgement, judgement, that is, founded on a rational, sincere and personal understanding, if not of the nature, of the existence of absolute value. For the preoccupations were not lived: only parts of them, scattered points of reference, had actually penetrated his life.

Now, a partial apprehension of his own experience is always dangerous for a public poet, who must be a moralist. It leads him into the blind alleys of hedonistic or didactic heresy down which Lowell so often travelled. When the rare success is achieved, it is achieved on a narrow front, though the result may be concentrated, powerful, overwhelming. But the insight is not self-sustaining.

In *Life Studies* Lowell examined and tested just this process of partial understanding and experience and traced his method to date to its root. He then began to rebuild or reconstruct his moral context. Almost every critic (and particularly those who have written illuminatingly about Lowell, which number include, at one time or another, almost every critic mentioned in these pages, even those I may have appeared to decry) has assumed that the process involved throughout was a demythologising, a depersonalising or an objectifying, of the poet's personality. In my submission it was not and to suggest that it was is to misunderstand both Lowell and the tradition of poetry in which he works.

In the degree to which self-questioning and self-doubt entered Lowell's career, it was directed towards discovering the place his personality occupied and ought to occupy, the role it played and ought to play, in his work. The general quality of a poet's work is, of course, determined by his ability, which includes the extent to which he can think clearly about himself and his motivations. Now, in the great successes of the first three volumes, though the poet's personality was brought in to sustain the poem, it was less powerfully present—in the way, that is, that I have suggested it is peculiarly present in English poetry since Johnson—than elsewhere in those volumes. In 'Colloquy in Black Rock' indeed, the personality receives and apprehends the Holy Ghost, but judges scarcely at all.

Now, for the sake of the greatest clarity I can achieve, I would like to re-state my belief about the place of the poet's personality in modern English poetry, for it is most important to be absolutely certain about this before dealing with *For the Union Dead*, where the doctrine is given embodiment in a new way. Of course the personality is in all poetry, in the sense that we recognise a good poem as the achievement of an individual: where difficulty arises in this area of understanding—as, perhaps, in the case of Homer—common sense can usually settle it without recourse to theory. More, we can usually, in dealing with a great or distinguished poet, recognise an individual and unique voice or tone, almost entirely his own and the product, one supposes, of his personality. This is the sense in which we sometimes might speak of Shakespearean, or Yeatsian or Eliotic quality, implying a quality unique to the named poet. There is, however, a sense in which such personalised adjectives are used only of poets whom we find very remarkable and, when used, imply the attainment by the poet named of something that resembles an immutable standard of achievement, some height that may be touched by other poets but the reaching of which we honour in some first exponent, by dubbing it, say, 'Shakespearean'. Thus Winters says of Stevens's 'Sunday Morning', and of its 'extraordinary subtlety' that 'I have compared this quality in Stevens to a similar quality in some of Shakespeare's sonnets'. He describes it as 'This particular kind of sensitivity' and suggests that 'at a lower level, or in another language and rhetorical tradition, it would probably display nothing that we should think of as Shakespearean'. There is thus the lurking sense that a distinct note in great poetry is the attainment of an objective success, outside the poet. Nonetheless, in common practice we do regard the poem as a personal achievement and the way in which that regard is framed was probably best summarised in Mr. Sparrow's formula: when we think of a work of art as great, he says, 'there is always a suppressed protasis in our thought: "This is a great work *if and in so far as it is the sincere product of a single mind*".'

All this is, I think, clear and acceptable enough. I set it out at length only because, in advance of discussing *For the Union Dead*, I want to be as clear as possible about the distinction between the way we commonly (and, in my opinion, fairly) think about the personality of the poet in relation to his achievement and the particular and positive way in which, in my opinion, the personality of the poet acts increasingly as an agent of synthesis in modern poetry.

In my view, then, the situation has arisen over earlier ages in which the poet is forced increasingly to openly add the force of his personal conviction to the argument of his poem because, for whatever reason, he feels that certain cultural resources are no longer available to him: he uses, as it were, the passionate force of himself to close the gaps in his argument. This is a uniquely modern, that is, post eighteenth century, situation. It has become virulent and potentially destructive on a wide scale in the twentieth century.

This can be put in another way. Let us say that the modern poet is increasingly unlikely to inherit a moral discipline. Whatever elements of such a discipline may attend him, nonetheless, he is forced to apply almost naked instinct, the barest and most unsupported promptings of his spirit, to the materials of his experience in the attempt to discover and elucidate value and discriminate between happenings. He must at one and the same time create a discipline for his personality *and* create or re-create a context of moral reference for his work. Now, to do this the poet must obviously pass through a period in which he comes to understand the basic elements of his own personality: that is, the quality and promise of his basic intellectual, moral and spiritual make-up, his genetic or inherited characteristics, the qualities that make him unique as an individual and the merit these qualities had in the business of writing poetry. Ultimately, the poet must know himself.

This we deduce. It is by no means necessary for the poet to communicate his self-examination to us, though one of the things that makes Lowell especially fascinating as a subject is the way in which he has shown us much of his own process of self-scrutiny. It is the next stage, however, which is important. The poet must show his capacity to create a moral context outside himself, must demonstrate the ability to discern value in experience and convince us of the rightness of his discernment in the argument of his poetry. If his personality still appears—and in the last poems of Yeats it appears more aggressively and triumphantly than ever before—it must be placed in relation to the context, that is, it must be seen about its work of discernment and discrimination: it is to be seen re-creating the moral context. It is to be seen—if an historical neologism may be forgiven—going through again something like the process of moral evolution and learning about value that mankind went through up to the point before which it became necessary to interject the personality into poetry.

In *Land of Unlikeness, Lord Weary's Castle* and *The Mills of the Kavanaughs* Lowell was working out the relationship between personality and acquired and inherited systems of value. The three great poems of this period have an almost archaic look about them because they represent near success in excluding the obvious activity of the personality. (Something of the same phenomenon can, of course, be seen in other poets, for instance, in Stevens, but here again achievement of this kind is rare. It can be seen more commonly in minor than in major poetry in our time.) Lowell's situation in this period was dangerous because he could not assent fully to the *rationale* of his various systems which were often in conflict with one another and he was thus, theoretically at any rate, in danger of being swallowed up by one of them.

In *Life Studies* Lowell progressed from disaster of a peculiarly self-willed kind to a near triumph of self-knowledge and self-discipline. The ground was thus cleared, but the balance was still precarious, in 'Skunk Hour'. The nature and quality of the personality was established as far as it could be without a context; the next task was the establishment of the context.

I want now to turn, in the light of these remarks, to the best poem in *For the Union Dead*, the title poem, which concludes the volume. The subject of this poem is the physical dismantling of old Boston in the interests of a new and savage urban order. That is taken to represent the destruction of order in a deeper civic and moral sense. In the first phase of his career Lowell would probably have seen the destruction—without necessarily being able to characterise it—and used it as the basis from which to issue an

apocalyptic denunciation. In this poem, however, he tries to do
three things; to characterise both the new and the superseded
order; to give the former the tribute of being organised and
hence substantial as well as evil, while offering similarly a charac-
terisation of the past order as well, which describes its value; and—
this being the most ambitious stroke of all—to surpass both
visions in an undertaking of true and immutable order which is
given reality in the poet and the poem.

This is a highly sophisticated and mature achievement. It is well
to note precisely what is achieved before scrutinising the text, both
in relation to this poem and in relation to what went before. In the
first phase of his career Lowell identified past and present in a
common corruption. Here he distinguishes between past and
present. But, in doing so, he makes interior distinctions as well.
He suggests, not that the whole of the modern world is condemned but that an organised capacity for evil is increasingly pre-
dominant in modern society. That evil is delineated not only in
respect of itself—in respect, that is, of its objective and obvious
character—but in respect of a better past as well, a past in which
the struggle for moral order was more pronounced. The important point is thus established that earlier New England (and
earlier America) had distinct moral aspirations. These are not,
however, regarded uncritically and the poem is thus rescued
from antiquarian sentimentalism.

Thus far, however, the argument has reached only the comparison between a better and a worse order. What transforms this
simple comparison is the presence of the poet himself in the poem,
the way in which, recognising his weakness for assertion as well
as his temptation to abandon the search for true order, he is able to
go through each of the scenes and experiences in the poem and
weigh and assess them, selecting what is and discerning what is
not, relevant to the order he is trying to define. Lowell learns value
as he goes along and so involves us in his activity, which results in
the erection of his poem as, in its capacity for discrimination and
judgement, the best modern symbol of an ultimate moral order.

In some ways, finally, this is the most serious and ambitious, as
well as being the most obviously so, of Lowell's public poems.

What he offers here is an individually created symbol of order; in doing so he takes the considerable burden of Laureateship on his shoulders and makes considerable claims for the importance and value of art and literature. Colonel Shaw's statue, which is in many respects the pivot of the poem is, like his own work, an artifact. It symbolises a value precisely defined and weighed in the poem. The death of awareness of the value is followed by the isolation (and, presumably ultimate destruction) of the statue as a work of art embodying that value. It is replaced, however, by a superior monument, the poem itself, as a symbol of the quality of the poet's judgement.

The poem consists of seventeen four-line stanzas of predominantly the same formal pattern with strictly controlled variations. The first stanza describes the old South Boston Aquarium, now deserted and desolate. The aquarium serves for an image of Boston and of society. Its outward structure was the order and discipline containing humanity. In the next stanza the poet, placing himself on the outside of experience, recalls his past practice and his present attitude to it:

> Once my nose crawled like a snail on the glass;
> my hand tingled
> to burst the bubbles
> drifting from the noses of the cowed, compliant fish.
>
> My hand draws back.

A past practice is thus judged no longer appropriate. Two things are worth noting here. One is the stanza break by which the completion of the statement is delayed and thereby given greater impact: this is used again with great effect later in the poem. The other is the poet's attitude to humanity. He is not recoiling from his previous judgement, merely finding his authority to make it, and hence its validity, no longer adequate. Combined with the stanza break this statement is given great point by the change in tense:

> Things thought too long can be no longer thought.

The next line and a half of the second stanza recall Lowell's regret for his past in 'the dark downward vegetating kingdom/of the fish and reptile'. This I take to stand, not only for humanity, but for the style of his past poetic practice and, indeed, within his new, flatter formal pattern, the words have a distinct ring of the early Lowell, contained and judged in the new style.

The remainder of the third and the next three stanzas describe the urban state of contemporary Boston and shift into the new theme of Colonel Shaw. The fifth stanza, except for the introduction of the word 'Puritan', is purely illustrative. The end of the third, and the whole of the fourth, stanzas are crucial:

> One morning last March,
> I pressed against the new barbed and galvanized
>
> fence on the Boston Common. Behind their cage,
> yellow dinosaur steamshovels were grunting
> as they cropped up tons of mush and grass
> to gouge their underworld garage.

As a description of purely mechanical activity the lines are unexceptionable. The overtone implies precisely what it is in modern Boston that Lowell is attacking: the overwhelming power of its mechanisation. In the sixth stanza he goes on to show one undoubted effect of the steamshovels' activity, the fact that the Civil War memorial to Colonel Shaw and his negro infantry has to be

> propped by a plank splint against the garage's earthquake.

The memorial, then, is still there, but its position has become precarious. The following stanzas define what the statue stands for and the relation between it, its value and the modern mechanistic landscape. By the end of the sixth stanza we are becoming involved in Lowell's descriptions, in their acceptability and validity, but we have only a general idea of where the argument is going, not a precise idea of its terms. We have also been given (in the second and third stanzas) a general idea of the poet's impulses, but we have also been told that he finds them not wholly

satisfactory, with the accompanying hint that he proposes to
attempt to frame a more appropriate, more discriminating
judgement.

The seventh stanza gives us an indication of what Lowell thinks
the relationship between men and the artifacts he makes should be;
its last line shows Lowell discriminating exactly about the
relationship:

> at the dedication,
> William James could almost hear the bronze Negroes breathe.

There is a delicate exactness and sense of reality about the scene
described. Its sense of the true transmission of sensory experience
establishes the physical context within which the real point of the
line is made. That point is that monuments to aspiration can *suggest* conduct to men, but not condition it. True, they suggest
value, but they cannot themselves teach it. Their relevance is thus
limited and (the point is made in the fourteenth stanza:

> There are no statues for the last war here;)

it is not the monument itself that enshrines value; rather it is the
capacity of man to continue to testify to the existence of aspiration
by erecting appropriate monuments that shows his awareness of
enduring value. This point is made critically: that is part of its
beauty; 'almost' shows the ultimate incommunicability by the
statue (the past) of what it stands for; 'bronze' versus 'breathe'
underlines that the statue embodies a message we must seek out
for ourselves; the past alone is not the truth.

Nonetheless, Colonel Shaw's past represents a better order than
Boston's presence:

> Their monument sticks like a fish bone
> in the city's throat.

In the next four stanzas Lowell describes Shaw and his men, their
appearance, actions and characteristics, and their America. It is
worth noting, however, that the words he chooses have a clear,

sharp tang about them and contrast with the clogged, violent words of the earlier stanzas.

> He has an angry wrenlike vigilance,
> a greyhound's gentle tautness;
> he seems to wince at pleasure.
> and suffocate for privacy.

The theme is generalised in the eleventh stanza:

> On a thousand small town New England greens,
> the old white churches hold their air
> of sparse, sincere rebellion; frayed flags
> quilt the graveyards of the Grand Army of the Republic.

Essentially, these stanzas are a salutation; they set, to an extent, a standard of judgement, valid because so precisely and accurately defined by the poet; valid also because entirely human, in contrast to the animalistic and mechanistic images of the second to the fifth stanzas.

The twelfth stanza continues the description, generalising it to cover other monuments and, particularly, to include the Union infantry. The thirteenth, and the first line of the fourteenth, stanzas (the second stanza break) return the past to the present:

> Shaw's father wanted no monument
> except the ditch,
> where his son's body was thrown
> and lost with his 'niggers'.

> The ditch is nearer.

This is a very powerful, and a very grave and measured, line. To Shaw's father's wish it adds a terrifying contemporary dimension. The ditch—the brutal fact of destruction of order—is very near now. This is not simply because of the yellow steamshovels. The true reason is given in the next line

> There are no statues for the last war here;

That is not simply (as the next passage makes clear) because of deeds done in the last war, but because the doing of those deeds demonstrated the death of aspiration in man. It is the inner corruption that is significant: the illustrations that follow demonstrate at a grave and then at a fiercely ironic level, the effects of that inner corruption; Lowell is distinguishing between surface and inner reality; the new mode, predicted in the second and third stanzas, is established:

> The ditch is nearer.
> There are no statues for the last war here;
> On Boyleston Street, a commercial photograph
> Shows Hiroshima boiling
>
> over a Mosler Safe, the 'Rock of Ages'
> that survived the blast. Space is nearer.
> When I crouch to my television set,
> the drained faces of Negro school-children rise like balloons.

There is an obvious internal irony in the lines about the safe. There is a further ironic contrast between the mute safe that 'survived'— an artifact—and the other artifact—the monument—that transmits value. As a monument, the safe also, of course, transmits: in its present context it transmits Hiroshima.

To elucidate the second last stanza we must return to the tenth, a part of the descriptive framework surrounding Shaw and a summary of the previous stanzas about the monument, but hitherto ignored:

> He is out of bounds now. He rejoices in man's lovely,
> peculiar power to choose life and die—
> when he leads his black soldiers to death,
> he cannot bend his back.

The first sentence distances and places the monument. The next line and a half contain a positive ambiguity. Shaw is, for the first time, given a personal capacity for feeling. He expresses the difference between his time and Lowell's: for him it was possible to choose life (value, aspiration) and die (in battle) without contradition; Lowell's contemporaries have the same power, but have chosen to die, to be dead to value, in a deeper and more profound sense. The next two lines again distance both Shaw and the monument: the Colonel cannot bend his back because of his integrity; the monument cannot because it is a monument—it cannot transmit.

The second last stanza also refers back to the bubbles in the second. It reads:

> Colonel Shaw
> is riding on his bubble,
> he waits
> for the blesséd break.

This is the second personalisation of Colonel Shaw. In it Lowell bids farewell to the continuing general commemorative value of the monument. The 'blesséd' break would activate his values again; that it will not come is shown by the designation of his hope as a bubble; as in the second stanza, the breaking of the bubble might unveil truth. The reason for the end of Shaw's hope is given in the fine last stanza, in which the significance of the breaking down of the containing walls of the Aquarium (representing order) and its consequences, are seen:

> The Aquarium is gone. Everywhere,
> giant finned cars nose forward like fish;
> a savage servility
> slides by on grease.

The beauty of this stanza lies not simply in the effect of the overall image, referring back as it does to the first and second stanzas; nor does it lie in the effect of release from confinement for the monsters that the lines achieve. It lies much more, first, in the way the sense of the last four lines denote escape while the syntax of the lines maintain tight and felicitous control over the description and, secondly, in the way in which this tight control stands for an ordered judgement—that is, a judgement founded on a just perception of order—established in the earlier part of the poem.

I want now to follow up Lowell's theme of revaluation in *For*

6

the Union Dead by turning to the third poem in which he uses Jonathan Edwards as both source and subject. This is 'Jonathan Edwards in Western Massachusetts' which, as Lowell says in his prefatory note, draws heavily on Edwards's prose.

'Western Massachusetts' returns, in a review of Edwards's career, to the theme of his teaching expressed in 'Mr. Edwards and the Spider': the occasion of the poem is a 'pilgrimage' to Northampton and so, though the inconsistencies of Edwards in thought and practice are gently and ironically pointed to, the purpose is serious and respectful. That moral purpose is to face up to and define the inadequacy of a faith once passionately and assertively believed in by both men, to face the consequences of abandoning the system of religion and to discover and weigh the human value of what is left. The meaning of the poem is quite clear. The truly absolute value, Lowell says, is self-knowledge, when it leads to humanity, towards oneself and others; it is perfectly compatible with religious vision and belief (the Sarah Pierrepont passages establish this and, incidentally, convey a uniquely personal religious vision far more effectively than Lowell ever managed to do for himself) but does not depend on it; it depends, ultimately, on man's knowledge of man, and of himself.

The first four stanzas depict the decline of the hellfire religion of which Edwards was a prime exponent; they also define what is left, the heritage, that has to be evaluated and point to the fact that advancing knowledge of man and his ways (the first line of the third stanza I quote refers to nuclear warfare) is one of the phenomena that has enabled Lowell to supersede Edwards's apprehension of the meaning of life. History has made the limitations of Edwards's philosophy apparent: the placing of Edwards in time involves the placing of his faith as well, for the decline of faith, the distance between man and his former God, is itself an objective proof, an account of the why as well as the how of the loss of faith. These are very beautiful, shimmering lines, they are also profoundly sad, for leave is taken of faith and the quest begun again for value, with a deep sense of the impermanence of human knowledge and the eternal intensity of striving for it.

I believe these four stanzas are among Lowell's finest achieve-ments (as, indeed, is the poem as a whole). I do not want to weary the reader with further protracted analysis, but I will quote the first four stanzas to give some idea of the quality of the whole and append a brief comment:

> Edwards' great millstone and rock
> of hope has crumbled, but the square
> white houses of his flock
> stand in the open air,
>
> out in the cold,
> like sheep outside the fold.
> Hope lives in doubt.
> Faith is trying to do without
>
> faith. In western Massachusetts,
> I could almost feel the frontier
> crack and disappear.
> Edwards thought the world would end there.
>
> We know how the world will end,
> but where is paradise, each day farther
> from the Pilgrim's blues for England
> and the Promised Land.

To a certain extent this reminds one of Stevens's 'Sunday Morn-ing'. The experience is more directly grim, less complex, than that of the poet in Stevens's great poem. Stevens, one might say, gains his encompassing strength from the calmness of wisdom, Lowell his from the calmness of a slightly grim stoicism. Wisdom is superior to stoicism and so Stevens is superior to Lowell: what they have in common seems to be a calm strength of vision. With Stevens, the only ultimate good is in the individual identity: maintaining that identity requires a combination of courage and calmness in the face of an underlying and encroaching terror, the terror of being unique and alone in the universe and then of being utterly destroyed by inevitable death. Two different passages from 'Sunday Morning' will convey the essence of the realised vision.

(For further analysis I invite the reader to turn to Yvor Winters's extraordinary essay on Stevens, perhaps the most brilliant piece of criticism written in this century):

> She dreams a little, and she feels the dark
> Encroachment of that old catastrophe,
> As a calm darkens among water-lights.
> . . .
> And, in the isolation of the sky,
> At evening, casual flocks of pigeons make
> Ambiguous undulations as they sink,
> Downward to darkness on extended wings.

This is to give the barest hint of Stevens's achievement, but it may suffice for the purposes of comparison with Lowell. If we return to the four stanzas quoted above their local excellences are easy to detect. There is an almost miraculous effect of precision achieved by the last line of the first stanza

> stand in the open air

—a line which, standing on its own, means nothing and conveys no quality. Alone and out of context it could not compare, for example to 'Faith is trying to do without', a line effective on its own and enjoying a meaning given an extra charge in the tragic irony of the first word of the next stanza 'faith', the stanza break itself creating the change. Yet, 'standing in the open air' completes the first stanza in a way, one feels, no other line could. Partly, this is a manifestation of formal metric control but it is also, one feels, more. It is evidence of moral control within the poet. Just as 'We know how the world will end' is the controlled, grim intrusion of a contemporary sensibility defined by the poet alone and representing a consciousness of evil and destruction both more immediate and more cosmic, more derived from the experience of every man, than was the consciousness of Edwards, so 'stand in the open air' is the irreplaceable, echoing conclusion because it is the line uniquely selected by Lowell in the changed context of the stanza that he selected it by a highly pressured but ultimately economic series of discriminations between experiences.

I will pass quickly over many excellent points in the poem to the stanzas where Lowell deals with Sarah Pierrepont and Edwards's love for her. Following the lines quoted above, we have three stanzas, set in italics, reviewing different senses of place and the immanence of God. Then four stanzas review the career of Edwards as a naturalist. Recalling his own poem 'Mr. Edwards and the Spider' Lowell points to the analogy Edwards drew between the mortality of man and that of the spider. The line 'You knew they would die' points back to his own line, 'We know how the world will end', subtly to underline the importance as well as the nature of the distance between Edwards's experience and his own. Edwards, Lowell is saying, derived from *his* environment, evidence for the significance of the inevitable death of individual man; Lowell derives from *his* evidence of the inevitable destruction of the species, an experience different in kind; one that bursts asunder the doctrines of Edwards and, as will become apparent later, moves man's spirit in a new direction, towards a stoical brotherhood of humanity, drawn together for comfort, in fear, yes, but in understanding also. I will anticipate, for a moment, to say that the resolution of the poem lies in the discovery that Edwards is also a member of that brotherhood, also a human being and worthy, and that the brotherhood can encompass and allow for his faith. The relationship between the two men is partly sustained by the use Lowell's poetry makes of Edwards's prose but more importantly by the fact that, while Lowell is trying to re-create the environment of faith in circumstances in which 'Faith is trying to do without/faith', that is, trying to make do within the quotidian apparatus of life and the monuments to the faith of the past, Edwards himself invested more of himself than he knew, and vastly more than was consistent with his doctrine, in human relations, in his love for Sarah.

It is one of the greatest strengths of the poem that Lowell is able to render Sarah's faith with a lyrical strength and compassion, a true conviction, that he never achieved during the days of his own faith, while also being able to absorb that account in his own scheme of things.

> So filled with delight in the Great Being,
> she hardly cared for anything—
> walking the fields, sweetly singing,
> conversing with some one invisible.

> Then God's love shone in sun, moon and stars,
> on earth, in the waters,
> in the air, in the loose winds,
> which used to greatly fix your mind.

This last ambiguously—but gently—ironic line allows Lowell to shift into a comparison of Edwards's life with Sarah and his doctrine and then to a further criticism of the doctrine itself. Several stanzas suggest the constriction the doctrine exercised on Edwards's humanity before Lowell bursts into his true identification with Edwards, seduced, afraid, dependent on an insignificant community as they depend on him

> I love you faded,
> old, exiled and afraid
> to leave your last flock, a dozen
> Houssatonic Indian children;

This beautiful climax reached Lowell, in a remarkable excess of bad taste, proceeds to destroy the whole effect in three and a half obtuse and irrelevant stanzas. These take up and particularize the theme, not of the stanza just quoted, but of the stanzas giving a generalised account of Edwards which precede it. Two stanzas, one from before, one from after, serve to make the point

> White wig and black coat,
> all cut from one cloth,
> and designed
> like your mind!
> . . .
> afraid to leave

all your writing, writing, writing,
denying the Freedom of the Will.
You were afraid to be president

(The presidency referred to is that of Princeton.) The poem could be saved in two ways: either the stanzas after 'Houssatonic Indian children' could be dropped, for they add little except footnotes of personal detail, or they could be worked in earlier in the poem and the Houssatonic children left to conclude it. As the thing stands, a potentially great poem is ruined.

Lowell's motive matters little in this assessment. It may have been that the final stanza is a failure of judgement pure and simple, the result of some fatal answering clumsiness in his mind that normally appears only in his cruder and more vulgar ironies and word plays. It may be, on the other hand, that these final stanzas are deliberate, designed. If so they have only one effect— to unload on to Edwards alone a burden the realised sharing of which has been, to this point, the finest achievement of the poem. Now, among writings on Lowell, Edwards's angular personality and even more angular doctrine has rarely been the object of considered sympathy. Indeed, I have already had occasion to record the suspicion that recoil from the man and his beliefs, inability to imagine that a twentieth-century poet could have entertained serious sympathy for so unsympathetic and inhumane a man and doctrine, has resulted in a serious underestimation and misinterpretation of 'Mr. Edwards and the Spider'. Nonetheless, the concluding stanzas of this poem cannot be imagined to be either just or appropriate by way of final *and concluding* response to Edwards. Even if, as a dreadful suspicion suggests, the poet's control has lapsed here and the resentment of Maule's Curse emerged once more, to assail with whimsical apostrophe a tradition for which the poet has very mixed feelings, it cannot but be bitterly regretted than an injustice to Edwards has led to such a sustained violation of the rest of the remarkable vision of the poem.

The failure here, however, may serve to show us one thing: how precarious the balance of even *For the Union Dead* is. Hitherto, in studying Lowell one has been shown, in his work, two dangerous fissures both of which appear, of course, in relation to, and as a result of the action on experience of, his personality. Ultimately, the personality of Lowell is crucially present in almost every poem, even when through reticence, pride or self-indulgence its precise operation is concealed from the reader. What has been won, by the minute persecution and evaluation of that personality by the time of *For the Union Dead* is won against the grain, against the dissatisfied inclination of the poet's personality. It has been won in spite of, as much as because of, that personality. By *For the Union Dead* the personality, the personal judgement, is under watchful and tight control most of the time rather than operating as a self-sustaining, fruitful and disciplined resource for poetry which it must be the ambition of Lowell eventually to make it. The fissures, then, are the product of the action of this flawed personality. They are, first, the partial subscription to doctrines which led Lowell to exaggerate the part at the expense of the whole and, second, the tendency to allow a self-indulgent interpretation of experience to masquerade as either objectivity or truth.

It is always useful to return to these main points in Lowell's development because they remind us effectively of the manner of that development and enable us to distinguish idiosyncrasy from achievement, more easily than we might otherwise manage. It is of the utmost importance that we distinguish between reference and achievement, as I argued at length in discussing 'The Quaker Graveyard in Nantucket' and 'The Mills of the Kavanaughs'. It is also important that we appreciate how (and therefore, in a sense, why) effects are contrived, and our appreciation of this phenomenon affects our estimation of the poem, as I suggested in discussing Wordsworth (above, p. 59f) Lowell's first fissure, over-commitment to a partial view of a given doctrine of life, whether heretical Catholicism or inhuman Puritanism—the vice of didacticism—is no longer a major feature of his work by the time of *For the Union Dead*. The other—the vice I have described as inverse hedonism—is still a potent and dangerous presence.

I discussed inverse hedonism at length in Chapter Four. In this chapter I want to relate it as much to Lowell's achievements as to

his failings though, to the latter end, I will return to the 'concluding passages of 'Jonathan Edwards in Western Massachusetts'.
However, in discussing the first four stanzas of that poem I stressed,
not only the individual achievement of the poem but the
generalisation of contemporary experience contained and
exemplified in the line 'We know how the world will end':
for Lowell that line is pregnant with both possibility and danger.

I will begin the illustration and elucidation of this statement
by referring to another of the very fine poems in *For the Union
Dead*, 'Fall 1961'. This poem has the same charged, precise style
as the others in this volume I have discussed. It discusses the world
political situation in the Autumn of 1961 and the possible
imminence of nuclear war (which was never in fact likely but
which was widely feared—the justified public concern which
Lowell uses) and its theme is the common helplessness and therefore common humanity of man in the face of a catastrophe of
total proportions and objective character. The sole instrument
of communication available to man is communication itself, that
is, talk, and talk is the least likely effective remedy for the private
individual: indeed, for him, its resources are already exhausted.
The second stanza reads:

> All autumn, the chafe and jar
> of nuclear war;
> we have talked our extinction to death.
> I swim like a minnow
> behind my studio window.

But

> The state
> is a diver under a glass bell.

The common predicament of humanity in the face of the
character of the weapon that threatens is more significant, more
all-embracing than any distribution of responsibility among men:
there is an analogy between state and individual. Lowell has now
gone through three stages of argument about death (it does not

matter if, chronologically, they overlap: the perception here is, in detail, more comprehensive than in 'Jonathan Edwards in Western Massachusetts'). In 'Mr. Edwards and the Spider' he traced the significance of death for each individual, but the shared inevitability led to no sort of human communion. In the early parts of 'Jonathan Edwards' that individual vision was transcended by a perception of the common predicament and the appropriate tragic reaction to it, which is rendered in the passage dealing with Edwards and the Houssatonic Indians. In 'Fall 1961' there is both a return and a development. The development is the exclusion, in the two lines last quoted, of individuals, at the helm of the state or not, from responsibility for the predicament: no blame, the cool, precise lines say, is attached. The return is in the objectivity which the development achieves. We are back with the Black Widow, but a just perception of contemporary experience teaches us that inevitable death may now be common, not just individual: commonality, in relation to the whole of humanity, replaces God, in relation to the individual, as the pivot of significance. It is the perception of this altered state of relations that justifies the supersession of the doctrine of Edwards. The poet's departure from that doctrine is thus objectified; his inclinations are reasoned out and thereby given authority.

Before discussing the general significance of this departure, I would like to proceed with the reading of 'Fall 1961'. Following the lines last quoted, we are reminded of two things. The first is (and this recall to reality is typical of Lowell at his best) that the predicament is nonetheless a predicament or a crisis for being viewed philosophically. Indeed, like the destruction of the civil order in 'For the Union Dead', the predicament has a unique and contemporary character, as shown in the way it overturns the natural order:

> A father's no shield
> for his child.

But the real point is the universality of the predicament, which is partly to be defined by the fact that the possibility of death by nuclear destruction for all—which is and should be, as realised in the lines just quoted, a critical, that is an immediate and unique, situation—has replaced 'death, simple death' as the common quotidian experience of mankind. This beautiful insight is conveyed in the next three lines

> We are like a lot of wild
> spiders crying together
> but without tears.

The spider reference does, of course, go back to 'Mr. Edwards and the Spider', but it is through the reference back, through 'crying together', that the change in range of perception is recorded and, as it were, in the poem as in life, realised. The final line completes a great insight, but one difficult to express in all its complexity.

It might be expressed thus. Individual death in relation to God was the most forceful insight into mortality available to Lowell. The meaning of that inevitable experience could be understood *by him* only by reference to a God he believed in but could not explain, a God distanced and divorced from any human perception, whose significance could only be stated and not argued. In a sense, and without disrespect, Lowell's awareness of death which dominated his representation of that vision was academic. With the passage of time another awareness of death became part of his everyday experience, an awareness he was capable of feeling because he had already been through other experiences of alienation and examination recorded in *The Mills of the Kavanaughs* and *Life Studies*. This was an awareness of death as total and communal, and, in its local character, nuclear. The difference in character of this perception from the earlier, God-related perception, completed his conversion from a God-centred philosophy in the traditional sense.

It remained to define the nature and significance of the newly-perceived death. Its nature lay in its total or communal character; its significance lay in the fact that it was potential, not inevitable. It is the totality of the potential destruction rather than its inevitability that sanctions the tense in 'Jonathan Edwards'. Potentiality rather than inevitability seems to me to be sanctioned by the double stanza coda to 'Fall 1961':

> Nature holds up a mirror.
> One swallow makes a summer.
> It's easy to tick
> off the minutes,
> but the clockhands stick.

> Back and forth!
> Back and forth, back and forth—
> my one point of rest
> is the orange and black
> oriole's swinging nest!

In these stanzas the poet returns to the rhythms and routines of his private world, sketched in the opening stanza. He also returns to the rhythms and routines of nature and the comfort they offer. The clinging together of humanity and, by extension, of natural life is the only available consolation.

Now I want to say another word about the mode of utterance in which these ideas, highly concentrated, are expressed: that mode is to be seen in the stanza form of all three poems I have been discussing. Run-over lines and stanza breaks, which I have already discussed, indicate that the object of the technique employed is to make of the stanza, or group of stanzas, one rhythmic unit, to achieve, that is, one of the most typical effects of the free verse movement. This technique harmonises exactly with the kind of moral discrimination which the poet is concerned to demonstrate and which I discussed above in terms of moral and spiritual control within his personality, particularly in relation to the first stanza of 'Jonathan Edwards'. The harmonisation is possible because of the way technical control is exercised. In each of these short stanzas we have two speech patterns running forward: the first is the pattern of ordinary day to day speech of an under-emphasised or laconic kind (this gives the impression of flatness to the verse, against which expressive words, 'white', 'alert', 'stand', 'open' stand out like landscape features, to be detected by the sensibility rather than the ear); the second of these running patterns is the iambic undercurrent of two syllable, unstressed and stressed, feet running forward with the ordinary speech rhythm.

Both of these patterns are flowing, that is, they move the poem forward from line to line, so that the traditional rhythmic break at the end of the line is faint or non-existent. This is principally what makes the stanza or group of stanzas, rather than the line, a rhythmic unit. In the first three stanzas of 'Jonathan Edwards' one notes that the only compulsory end-line break before the eleventh line comes in mid-stanza ('Hope lives in doubt'). It is followed by a declaratory line ('Faith is trying to do without') that, as I pointed out before, has a meaning in itself, but invites the completion of that meaning by a lurch across the stanza break. This point, indeed is the best one for demonstrating the way in which Lowell disciplines the forward run of speech and iambs:

Faith is trying to do without

faith. In western Massachusetts,

In isolation these two lines can be read as a single unit, if one ignores the full stop. Other readings and internal emphases can be seen more clearly when they are placed in context.

Isolating the lines, however, serves to show how the full stop acts as a brake on the iambic-sense flow: this is not a perfect example, but in general it may be said that, in addition to their ordinary sense function the full stops in Lowell's verse do serve this braking function. In doing so they reinforce the free verse stress system of the stanzas.

The free verse system Lowell uses is based on the single foot line, containing a primary and a secondary stress. This is varied by a number of longer, irregular lines, used usually to summarise or resume an argument or begin a new one. The irregularities, the variations, that is, from the basic structure of the verse make up the bridge between the iambic-sense flow and the stress pattern.

Because the basic line unit consists of two stresses, because that basic line is so short and because the basic metric unit of this kind of full verse is itself so short that it does not allow the lengthy development of more traditional metric systems, in which the elaborate rules of stress become clear, there is a hesitation, an ambiguity over which syllable should be stressed in a line. That hesitation is not meant to be resolved: in reading the poem aloud the reader should try to convey the ambiguity by checking his placing of the primary emphasis so as to suggest that an alternative stress is possible. It is extraordinarily difficult to do this at the same time as one is doing justice to the flow of the iambic-sense current and accounting for the run-over lines and stanza breaks as well.

The stresses thus act as a series of checks to the flow; the ambiguity of stress, if properly expressed, creates a living movement within the tension established between flow and checks. It is this combination, supported by, as I suggested earlier, an extraordinary tactility in the choice of words, that creates the remarkable shimmer of these lines—'shimmer' being taken to mean precisely the living shift of stress (which is a shift of meaning, since stress alters emphasis and thus sense) which occurs in the verse. Technically, this account of the system explains why the line 'stand in the open air' has the effect discussed earlier.

But earlier I said that that line and its effect demonstrated the inner power of moral control and discrimination in the poet. There is no contradiction. If we turn to the last five stanzas (one of them two line) in 'Jonathan Edwards', which I have so harshly criticised, we see that the stress ambiguity has become generalised: there is no hesitation between alternatives or suggestions as to which to choose. The structure is suddenly loose and the tension between iambic-sense flow and stress-check—the shimmer—is destroyed, as has been the right argument for the poem. Technical dissolution reflects rational and conceptual dissolution.

It is proper to devote more time to the technical features of *For the Union Dead* than to the technical features of the earlier volumes. This is because, as I suggested earlier, in the first phase of his career form was separated from argument in Lowell's practice; his use and adaptation of tradition forms was supplementary to his argumentation scheme, and when the two fused together it was accidental, in the sense that his early success bore that accidental look, seem, as it were, uniquely prominent in his work as a whole. As I have suggested, at that time, Lowell was trying to achieve poetry by various experimental mixes of elements of fact, doctrine, history, experience and form. When a success was achieved, however, the mixture did not become a formula, in an obvious sense because there was always a unique element in it— a quotation or reference, maybe, or a pattern of words or perceptions taken from someone else—in a deeper and more profound sense because Lowell himself was in doubt about the true nature of his system of belief, about the real characteristics of the moral context he was working in.

In *Life Studies* the moral context of the poet was put under reconstruction and the job, at least in relation to the larger verities, was completed in *For the Union Dead*. The form there is designed for that context. In discussing 'For the Union Dead', for example, I suggested that the poem itself was an artifact symbolising right order, replacing Shaw and opposing contemporary Boston. It was, in effect, a new monument. That statement was reflected, not only in the argument of the poem, but in its structure, in the tension and the shimmer. Similarly, in 'Jonathan Edwards' the great question posed is, what new order of value can be constructed out of the detritus of day to day life when the great synthesizing agent of religious doctrine has been taken away. The elements of the detritus are held, focused and moved around in different relationships, again by the structure. In 'Fall 1961' this structure serves the purpose of what we may think of as a peculiarly contemporary mode of consciousness. The stillness the formal system creates there achieves an effect somewhat analogous to that threatening stillness in the air which was felt in London during the closing stages of the last war when V–bomb motors suddenly shut off before the bomb came free-falling towards its target. A similar stillness, in both the physical and political atmosphere, was made the subject of a remarkable radio broadcast to England by Alistair Cooke during the Cuban missile crisis and something of the same effect may be seen when a film or television director freezes a frame and halts a film to make a particular point. Psychologically, the arrest of movement and the stillness defines the context of predicament.

There is yet a deeper purpose for Lowell in the use of this form: it is an objectifying, distancing form. It recalls, as it were, the work of the lepidopterist and the poem is saved from the frozen life of lepidoptery by the flow of iambics and speech through it, like the flow of blood through the veins. What Lowell is doing throughout these poems is sifting and learning from observation and experience, re-working and re-shaping phenomena into a moral system. That is why so many of the poems in *For the Union Dead*—all but those we have discussed—are, despite an often considerable achievement, minor, because so much experience and meaning has to be sifted and re-valued. The minor poems, as it were, stake out and define fairly small areas of experience and value; but when the phenomenon confronted is large enough, or when enough ground has been cleared, a large and over-mastering idea may take over and be worked out in a much more substantial poem.

Take, for example, two good poems in this volume, 'Water' and 'The Old Flame'. Both recall past time spent by the poet with a woman; in the second this is avowedly, in the first probably, the poet's wife (probably Lowell's first). Water describes the inter-action between people and environment in a landscape of fixed and clear beauty

> dozens of bleak
> white frame houses stuck
> like oyster shells
> on a hill of rock,

The poem is retrospective, too, in the sense that it recalls the transcendently apocalyptic modes of the earlier work and puts them by:

> One night you dreamed
> you were a mermaid clinging to a wharf-pile,

and trying to pull
off the barnacles with your hands.

We wished our two souls
might return like gulls
to the rock. In the end,
the water was too cold for us.

This is a sad, rather wistful, but strong and precise little poem.
'The Old Flame' recalls the Maine farmhouse where he and his
wife once lived. The first four stanzas are jolly; the third reads

Inside, a new landlord,
a new wife, a new broom!
Atlantic seaboard antique shop
pewter and plunder
shone in each room.

But in the remaining five stanzas the tone changes and shifts. The
wife's 'ghostly/imaginary lover' is seen at the window, but
exorcised by time and the new inhabitants:

Health to the new people,
health to their flag, to their old
restored house on the hill!
Everything had been swept bare,
furnished, garnished and aired.

'Everything's', as Lowell says, 'changed for the best'. But, through
the remaining three stanzas a fierce nostalgia, at odds with the
philosophy of this line, burns: 'How quivering and fierce we
were', the poet says before recalling

your old voice
of flaming insight
that kept us awake all night.
In one bed and apart,

This nostalgia is a note of strength, for it is only from a position of assurance that Lowell can afford to invoke fierce memories which he tames and orders in his syntax and by the inimitably memorial tone of his voice.

In the three major poems of the volume which we have examined, however, we can see the outline of the position Lowell has now adopted. The existence and threat of the nuclear weapon and the destruction of moral, symbolised in the destruction of civil order are his themes and material, enriched by his sense of the common human predicament and by the resources of his and man's past and culture. Lowell proceeds to judgement by deduction, by deducing value both from a reaction to what is happening and from the remains of past systems of value. This is an arduous proceeding for, to objectify his judgement, to rescue it from self-indulgence, he has to make judgements respectful of the variety of human nature and experience from facts. Earlier poets in the tradition, of course, deduced from value and judged facts in the light of rules for how to live. The value, the rules, the moral order, Lowell has to extract from dross.

In discussing Mr. Alvarez and other writers, and the method of Lowell himself, in the chapter on *Life Studies*, this modern difficulty was precisely what we were up against. The danger is that men will resolve their confrontation with facts (or apparent facts) by resource to their impulses rather than their reason. Moreover, the deduction from fact in terms of value (which is the characteristic task and difficulty of modern man) presents further problems which encourage this destructive obedience to impulse. A moral system (which it is the object to create) is a system of distinguishing between good and evil. That is its theological basis and religions, laws and politics all frequently claim the ability to make such distinctions. Poetry (and art generally) however, only make the claim that the distinction is possible. In art, moreover, the distinction is more sophisticated than I have suggested; it is, in fact, a system of distinctions, or discriminations which make of the individual poem a moral universe. Within the boundaries of common sense the poem makes its own laws, best summed up in the phrase describing the task as one of making 'an appropriate judgement on experience', where appropriate refers to the size and importance of the experience, the motives and capacity as well as intentions and beliefs of people involved in it and the moral quality—that is, the capacity to conceive and convince by description of a moral order—of the poet.

I say 'within the boundaries of common sense' because, of course, the poem reflects and is conditioned by, though ultimately independent *as an artefact* of, the moral order of the world outside. Furthermore, when the moral order of the world outside is unstable, poets (like Lowell) invariably seek to re-create it: from this experience I deduce that poetry testifies to the existence of absolute truths without which a moral order cannot exist. The problem is to define those truths.

The poem can as well be a search for the truth as truth itself, or it can be the expression of a limited truth. In the latter case, however, the range of the truth is also limited and so the response to experience may be as well. One of the difficulties Mr. Alvarez suffered from was the fact that, while the range of the evil detected by him was almost unlimited, the range of truth or good he could oppose to it was very severely limited indeed, and further limited by the fact that he declined to use his reason. Now I am of course aware that evil can, so to speak, turn the lines of truth: Lowell can plausibly imply in 'Jonathan Edwards' that the immediate experience of the existence of the nuclear weapon, in its impact on him, can make the theological doctrines Edwards entertained inadequate. This is of course the case, and it has happened very widely in the modern world. We are, however, less concerned with what particular kind of absolute truth, or absolute standard of good may exist, as with the resources available for poetry. If a theological absolute exists, that is, if a religious faith is available to the poet, then he is better equipped. Not so equipped he must close the gap between his range of value and the range of evil he sees with his judgement. That is, he must work to extend the scope of his reason; that is what Stevens does in 'Sunday Morning'; it is what Lowell does in For the Union Dead, with a great measure of success.

The difficulty about deducing from fact as opposed to from

value, however, is precisely this one of limited range and temporary applicability. It is much more difficult to sustain a conviction of the imminence of nuclear destruction and to use it over the years as a stable element in poetic thinking than it is to use, say, the Devil in a similar way. Yet to use it as a symbol of man's tendency to evil is also extremely difficult as, without a theological system, awareness of that tendency to evil must become either uselessly generalised (as it is with Mr. Alvarez and in some of the poems in *Life Studies*) or it must be re-argued from the beginning almost every time one writes a poem, and at the same time as the poet is trying to increase by rational development the range, scope and discrimination of his judgement.

This is the difficulty faced in *For the Union Dead* and it gives warning of the delicacy of the equilibrium of even the finest poems there. It may explain the collapse at the end of 'Jonathan Edwards'. It certainly accounts for the existence in the volume of a number of highly personal exploratory poems which discuss the nature of this problem. The final stanzas of 'Jonathan Edwards', of course, in shifting responsibility on to Edwards, are self-indulgent in the same way as are some of the poems I criticised in *Life Studies*. 'Alfred Corning Clark' in *For the Union Dead*, which laments the death of a rich friend, shows throughout a humorously self-deprecating consciousness, withdrawing from contest with the vulgar (if pleasant) world Clark comes from, which manifests, in its refusal to engage, a form of that self-indulgence. Though minor, it is however a good poem, because of the critical awareness of the situation the humour (and the affection in the lines) demonstrates and which alleviates the self-indulgence:

> There must be something—
> some one to praise
> your triumphant diffidence,
> your refusal of exertion,
> . . .
> You are dear to me, Alfred;
> our reluctant souls united
> in our unconventional
> illegal games of chess

on the St. Mark's quadrangle
You usually won—
motionless
as a lizard in the sun.

More directly the poem 'Eye and Tooth' shows Lowell's awareness of the problem described above. This is the poem that ends
with the famous line

I am tired. Everyone's tired of my turmoil.

This poem reviews Lowell's search for an unblemished Adam.
The first stanza uses his common image of a goldfish bowl to
convey helplessness. Roughly, the rest of the poem confesses the
stubborn refusal of his sensibility to abandon the insight into ruin
of his youth and the refusal to abandon, also, or to treat as a
mirage, the evidence he sees for that insight:

My eyes throb.
Nothing can dislodge
the house with my first tooth
noosed in a knot to the doorknob.

Nothing can dislodge
the triangular blotch
of rot on the red roof,
a cedar hedge, or the shade of a hedge.

In other words inner conviction tells him evidence is to be found
everywhere, in appearance as well as in reality. What makes this
poem successful, however, is that that view, which elsewhere
corrupts his work, is here controlled and disciplined, made tenta-
tive because personal. If, however, Lowell goes on, the vision is
true then there must be an equal, an adequate, a weighty response:
the failure to find it is the cause of his turmoil:

No ease from the eye
of the sharp-skinned hawk in the birdbook there,

> with reddish brown buffalo hair
> on its shanks, one ascetic talon
>
> clasping the abstract imperial sky.
> It says:
> *an eye for an eye,*
> *a tooth for a tooth.*
> . . .
> Nothing! No oil
> for the eye, nothing to pour
> on those waters or flames.
> I am tired. Everyone's tired of my turmoil.

This poem, of course, deals, not with the problem itself, but with the margins of the problem. What raises it above the common run is the acutely realised personal intensity of the account: Lowell is dealing not only with a public problem for the poet, but with a personal agony.

Most of the remaining poems in *For the Union Dead* deal either with this problem or with the recapitulation and revaluation of the past. Not all are successful, and some show deep flaws of self-indulgence, but nearly all have something to recommend them. In a weak poem, for example 'Caligula', Lowell manages to deal with dignity and perception with something of the same problem that confronted Mr. Alvarez:

> Your true face sneers at me, mean, thin, agonized,
> the rusty Roman medal where I see
> my lowest depths of possibility.

and

> Animals
> fattened for your arena suffered less
> than you in dying—yours the lawlessness
> of something simple that has lost its law,
> my namesake, and the last Caligula.

Here in 'something simple that has lost its law', is the essence of the matter.

Both 'Night Sweat' and 'The Flaw' extend exploring tentacles towards possible sources of comfort. These two poems have something of the manic disruptions of parts of *Life Studies* and the new discipline is not always successful in containing them. 'Night Sweat' returns to the personal fear of inability to write and judge as, again, obsessionally symbolised by tidiness and garnished rooms, as places from which inspiration has gone:

> Work-table, litter, books and standing lamp,
> plain things, my stalled equipment, the old broom—
> but I am living in a tidied room,

But out of disturbance and disruption comes a critical lyric, one that makes a moving appeal to his wife who, despite sharing the weakness of all that is flesh may be a source, not of comfort only, but of value. The sudden peace of these lines is moving:

> my wife . . . your lightness alters everything,
> and tears the black web from the spider's sack,
> as your heart flops and flutters like a hare.
> Poor turtle, tortoise, if I cannot clear
> the surface of these troubled waters here,
> absolve me, help me, Dear Heart, as you bear
> this world's dead weight and cycle on your back.

Similarly, at the end of 'The Flaw':

> Dear Figure curving like a questionmark,
> how will you hear my answer in the dark?

Even when faulty these poems, and almost all of *For the Union Dead*, represent, in my view, the most substantial advance of Lowell's career and its most nearly self-sustaining achievement. His problem—the problem of the modern poet—is here extraordinarily precisely delineated and the equipment for the task in hand is impressively in evidence. I have suggested that the task, especially given Lowell's ambition, is still very great and that its nature makes the equilibrium achieved precarious. What is

present throughout, however, is an astonishing critical determination, in thought and technique, which sifts experience and
informs and dominates the work. Lowell refuses any longer to
go along with systems of thought or doctrine the validity of
which he has not lived and, most important of all, if he has not
got the impulses of his personality fully under control, he does
know precisely what its role should be in his public work. The
achievement has principally been to see himself and his task
steadily and whole.

6 Near the Ocean and Imitations

AT THE END of *For the Union Dead*, then, Lowell had achieved both a new mind of argument and a new style, the latter a disciplined development from the loose structures of *Life Studies*, themselves a deliberate breakdown of the formal patterns of the first phase of his career. In that new rhythm the stresses acted as halting counterpoints to the flow of an iambic pattern, in which the stanza or group of stanzas, not the line, was the rhythmic unit. We had thus a system of *measure*—the iambic pattern whose skeleton could be perceived—counterpointed by a *cadence*; the purpose of the cadence was to expose and emphasise the stress of particular words and phrases. Now, stress is normally laid on a syllable. What Lowell achieved with his hybrid system was an extension of syllabic stress and a creation of a kind of moral stress. Thus, in the line I have already had occasion to quote as an example, 'stand in the open air', one can stress 'stand' and 'open', thus making the line iambic with one slack or unstressed syllable or 'outride', to use Hopkins's word. But this gives an altogether inadequate account of the place the line occupies in the stanza. If one allows one's ear to hear the lines simply as free verse based on the iamb, one misses the explanation of the total effect of the verse. One misses, that is, what I have called the 'shimmer', or rather one fails to detect how the shimmer is achieved. One notices it, of course; no moderately sensitive ear could fail to, but one may fail to understand why it is there and, indeed many critics who have commented on the rather mysterious quality of many lines in *For the Union Dead* have not gone on to attempt an account of it in technical terms, though they usually mention its onomatopoeia. Now, onomatopoeia and the verbal texture it helps to produce are far too often discounted or given insufficiently systematic discussion in criticism nowadays, perhaps because they form so large and simple a part of the corrupt

Romantic notions of what poetry is which dominates our schools. Nonetheless, despite this general point, onomatopoeia does not play a substantial or distinctive part in Lowell's later verse.

I have recapitulated and slightly extended this technical account because it is a suitable preface to the next stage in Lowell's technical development, which we must reach through an account of the technical limitations (not deficiencies) of *For the Union Dead*. One other positive point must be made: it is often contended that running rhythm on the traditional pattern provided the most effective foil or counter to speech or sense stress. Conversely, it is maintained, spring rhythm (which combines poetic and speech or sense stress; Gerard Manley Hopkins coined the phrase and was the most distinctive practitioner of the method; the system in *For the Union Dead* is descended directly from his practice) affords no such system of counterpoint. That is not strictly true, or, at least, it does not tell the whole story. What Lowell achieved in *For the Union Dead* was a system of counterpoint; it was not, however, a system of tension between rhythm and speech but between *obvious speech pattern* and the *internal possibilities of speech*.

This is an absolutely crucial point and one best made at the point where the development of *For the Union Dead* leaves off and the development of *Near the Ocean* takes over. It is, as will become clear, closely involved with the discussion of moral theory underlying the structure of poetry in the last chapter. I would like, therefore, to take some trouble to make it absolutely clear, or as nearly clear as I can manage.

I have made the point (particularly in the discussion of 'For the Union Dead') that, with Lowell, the poem becomes a more independent system of moral order in itself than we are accustomed to thinking of it as being. By 'more independent', I mean that the poem and the poet, being victims of the historical development described in my first chapter, can rarely call for substantive assistance on comprehensive moral unanimities; the good poem, therefore, must depend on a more intricate system of independent reasoning. I do not want to imply, of course, that the poets of earlier ages were able to accept shibboleths uncritically: indeed, the very act of subjecting an experience or an idea to the test of the concentrated force of good poetry is to subject it to the finest criticism imaginable. Nor am I absolutely certain (I expressed reservations in my first chapter) that it is more difficult to write good poetry in the twentieth century (as a general principle) than earlier, though I share the view that literature has been in general decline for a very long time. It may be, for example, that, dominated as we all are by various kinds of educational detritus, we, and the poets, need rather to re-learn our methods of presenting ancient truths. It may be, of course, that our civilisation is in a decline that cannot be arrested, and that the methods will not be re-learned. To some extent, however, 'Waking Early Sunday Morning', the first poem in *Near the Ocean*, and perhaps Lowell's greatest, supports the former point.

Let us, therefore, abandon the theoretical discussion of alternatives and return to the general points I have made about the poem and the personality of the poet in general and the task facing Lowell in *For the Union Dead* in particular. What was going on in that volume, it seems to me, was a general revaluation of experience and belief, carried on in such a way as to isolate and present certain general propositions. The new style of the better poems in the volume was suited exactly to that purpose. It was a style of great precision, but of limited range, both philosophically and technically. Within those limits, each line was crammed with meaning, each phrase, and almost each word, was exploited to the full, while the tight discipline of both argument and style greatly reduced (and often eliminated) the dangers of general impressionistic ambiguity which so damaged Lowell's earlier work. The vital point to remember is that the exploitation and the avoidance of unproductive ambiguity were due as much to the form as to the argument (though, presumably, the poet would not have developed the form unless he wanted to present the argument). The resources of literary reference, for example, are scarcely used in *For the Union Dead* in the way they were used earlier, that is, for their multiple meaning, as in the lines from 'The Mills of the Kavanaughs'.

That is in large part, not simply the renunciation of the kind of impressionistic ambiguity as to the meaning and significance the poet is according to quotations and references, but because that kind of effect cannot be achieved, or can only be achieved in a very limited way, while using a style like that in *For the Union Dead*, a style which concentrates stress and emphasis on the potentialities of words reflecting sense phenomena, not literary resource or erudition. This development in Lowell has a general significance beyond his own work: in his earlier poetry—though appearance might superficially suggest the contrary—Lowell was deeply influenced by the school of Pound and Eliot. From their school and their influence derives his system of literary reference with moral overtones, an impressionistic, ambiguous system that works to conceal such truth as the poet has access to. Lowell's abandonment of the system may presage a more general flight.

There are, nonetheless, severe limitations of thought and action in *For the Union Dead*. Before dealing with them, however, I would like to say one more word about the merits of this form, about its historical context and about the reaction to it of good criticism. The style of the best work in the volume injects significance into ordinary words, makes one feel, as I suggested earlier, that the poet has been about a business of strenuous selection and that, therefore, the words are important, are significant. The tight disciplined style may make us appreciate the presence of significance without comprehending its nature. The effect, therefore, is one of mystery.

This contrived—or perhaps it would be better to say, 'designed' —air of mystery in much of modern poetry was the object of some of the sternest strictures of Yvor Winters. It was what he characterised as most typically modern and most typically decadent. In the strict sense he was correct, as he was in almost all of the judgements on individual poets, arising out of this general point, in *In Defense of Reason*. But it is not, I feel, enough merely to demonstrate the fault in the method and in its application. Winters may have missed, I feel, two things. He may have missed the argument, turmoil and ambition that went into the devising of the method, so integral to Yeats's work. And he may have missed its general relevance for poetic practice, its attempt on those very heights of moral objectivity from which Winters looked down. An air of mystery, slight or considerable, may be merely a sign that something like the process of debate I have described in this and the last chapter is going on. It may, as I have suggested many times in this book, conceal an unwillingness or inability to judge; it may, as I have suggested many times in these chapters, be a stage in the ferment from which a new poetic language may emerge. Winters was, I believe, insufficiently alive to these possibilities, which is not, of course, at all the same thing as saying he was wrong in his judgements.

This paragraph may have given some hint of the limitations I have to find in *For the Union Dead*. I have suggested that the volume saw the operation of a system of tension between obvious speech pattern and the internal possibilities of speech. It is precisely those internal possibilities that remain mysterious. *For the Union Dead* does not have the ultimate complexity of really great poetry, though it does have the mystery which is sometimes a surface manifestation of that complexity. The central theme of each of the really fine poems in that volume can be stated quite simply and without reduction. What cannot be summarised is the mood, that is, the context, within which the theme is presented. But the theme is a theme, the mood a mood and the context a context. The latter supports the former but is not part of it, except in the occasional line or stanza. What the poet has done is create a mood which is an appropriate one for him, within which he can feel the significance of the theme. The form supports the argument, but the fusion between them in limited. It is as though—though this is not quite fair when one thinks of the whole work—the poet is saying 'On such and such a day I felt this' rather than 'Like all other arguments this one demonstrates this truth'. Uniqueness, then, or an impression of it, is cultivated: what saves the poetry from being minor is the size of the theme, confidently handled, and the disciplined impact of the personality felt in the act of strenuous choice and discrimination.

Nonetheless, the limitation remains. It is the limitation that has plagued Lowell all his life, the limitation of annunciatory poetry. Everything is but a preparation for the statement of the overmastering idea and, consequently, the suspicion arises that the stage has been too carefully set. The idea does not live in the lines, but only in some of them; it is a mood appropriate to the idea that lives in the lines. That this does not lead to disaster is because of the presence of the elements mentioned in the last paragraph. The form is integral to the presence of those elements; it is also, with its very even and local stresses, with the way the activity and movement of those stresses is confined, integral to the limitation. The limitation is that an idea and a scene only, not an experience and a judgement on it, can be expressed within this form. In 'Jonathan Edwards in Western Massachusetts' the line 'We know how the world will end' is ironically and appropriately intruded but its weight comes entirely from reflective ratiocination, from 'recollection in tranquillity', rather than from the fusion of experience, responses and judgement.

In saying this I do not want to be misunderstood. In implying that a kind of fusion is lacking I do not imply that the form should express the matter. Not at all: that is a wildly common simplification of the true nature of the relationship between form and argument and is to be found everywhere an element in poetry— the reflection of meaning in sound—is exclusively cultivated to the point that the highest—and often only—praise of a work lies in an estimation of the degree to which sound reflects meaning. I mean, rather, this: a poem consists of the description of an argument or of an experience rendered as argument, in a manner subject to the discipline of form. Form is not there to express either the experience or the argument but to communicate the judgement the poet is making on them. Form is, therefore, as I have said before, a demonstration of moral control and discrimination within the poet. The difficulty of its relation to—or fusion with—matter arises because poetry is a concentrated kind of speech as form is a concentrated kind of judgement and that concentration, of argument and form, embraces connotation (the history and the emotional power of words) and denotation (their grammatical meaning). The relationship is not, therefore, between form and matter but between two different kinds of concentration of thought, both capable of expressing a wider (but more controlled) range of meaning than prose, capable, that is, of concentrating the rational and the emotional and of judging the appropriateness of the one to the other. That is fusion. Because the concentration of the emotional and of the rational are so often separated in *For the Union Dead*, it takes place in that volume only intermittently. Finally—and this is a crucial point, as central to my general argument as the earlier discussion of unique; absolute and objective (p. 90f)—such separation of the elements of fusion, on occasions when the other characteristics of good poetry are present, is commonly an indication that the poetry under scrutiny is of *the middle order of achievement*.

The point may still seem elusive and I will try to illustrate it. The great danger seems to me to be one of confusion between my account of the relationship between form and matter and the account that suggests that form expresses matter—the Eliotic account. Let us confine our examples to the modern period for the sake of reasonable brevity, though to do so implies an elevation of Lowell higher than in my considered judgement. Here is a passage from Eliot's *Four Quartets*

> The sea howl
> And the sea yelp, are different voices
> Often together heard: the whine in the rigging,
> The menace and caress of wave that breaks on water,
> The distant rote in the granite teeth,
> And the wailing warning from the approaching headland
> Are all sea voices, and the heaving groaner
> Rounded homewards, and the seagull:
> And under the oppression of the silent fog
> The tolling bell
> Measures time not our time, rung by the unhurried
> Ground swell, a time
> Older than the time of chronometers, older
> Than time counted by anxious worried women
> Lying awake, calculating the future,
> Trying to unweave, unwind, unravel
> And piece together the past and the future,
> Between midnight and dawn, when the past is all deception,
> The future futureless, before the morning watch
> When time stops and time is never ending;

> And the ground swell, that is and was from the beginning,
> Clangs
> The bell.

Here form expresses matter. In her sympathetic and influential commentary Dr. Helen Gardner comments: '. . . *Four Quartets* is unique and essentially inimitable. In it the form is the perfect expression of the subject; so much so that one can hardly in the end distinguish subject from form'.[1] Just so.

But poetry is not an instrument of expression: it is an instrument of judgement. Eliot reflects experience; he demonstrates, not principles but attachment to principles; and his sense of tragedy is diffuse and indulgent, a matter of mood rather than thought.

Here is a single passage, in a flawed poem, by Stevens:

> I am a man of fortune greeting heirs;
> For it has come that thus I greet the spring.
> These choirs of welcome choir for me farewell
> No spring can follow past meridian.
> Yet you persist with anecdotal bliss
> To make believe a starry connaissance
> —*Le monocle de mon Oncle*

Here, surely, is control, not expression, and achievement of a different order. And now, 'Sunday Morning'

> She says, 'I am content when wakened birds,
> Before they fly, test the reality
> Of misty fields, by their sweet questionings;
> But when the birds are gone, and their warm fields
> Return no more, where, then, is paradise.'

The control, the judgement, lies in the form which conveys the unique experience, objectively expressed, of an absolute truth. There is fusion, but not limitation.

And Yeats, about the same task of penetrating the truth behind appearance and experience:

Suddenly I saw the cold and rook-delighting heaven
That seemed as though ice burned and was but the more ice,
And thereupon imagination and heart were driven
So wild that every casual thought of that and this
Vanished, and left but memories, that should be out of season
With the hot blood of youth, of love crossed long ago;
And I took all the blame out of all sense and reason,
Until I cried and trembled and rocked to and fro,
Riddled with light. Ah! when the ghost begins to quicken,
Confusion of the death-bed over, is it sent
Out naked on the roads, as the books say, and stricken
By the injustice of the skies for punishment?

—The Cold Heaven

I have not selected the best of any of the three poets, but rather
familiar passages, much commented upon. I will observe, merely
as a point of reference in my general argument, what there
would be little point in demonstrating here, that the lines from
Eliot are from the line of wit; those of Yeats in manner from the
line of gravity, in matter ambiguous; and those of Stevens
ambiguous in their derivation in both matter and manner: both
the latter thereby achieve moments of comprehensiveness
ultimately Shakespearean, which defeat a critical policy of
division or exclusion. About the first and last stanzas of Lowell's
'Waking Early Sunday Morning' there is no ambiguity of intent:

O to break loose, like the chinook
salmon jumping and falling back,
nosing up to the impossible
stone and bone-crushing waterfall—
raw-jawed, weak-fleshed there, stopped by ten
steps of the roaring ladder, and then
to clear the top on the last try,
alive enough to spawn and die.
. . .
Pity the planet, all joy gone
from this sweet volcanic cone;
peace to our children when they fall
in small war on the heels of small

war—until the end of time
to police the earth, a ghost
orbiting forever lost
in our monotonous sublime.

Here is control of experience, not reflection of phenomena or feeling.

It is, I think, instantly obvious from these lines how Lowell has progressed from *For the Union Dead* and how his range has increased. The longer line and the more fluent system of stress greatly increases the encompassing capacity of the form. In the lines I quoted from Eliot we can see fine local precision, in an indecisive, slack, unconcentrated framework. In *For the Union Dead* local precision is admirably ordered within a precise and decisive intellectual framework (particularly in 'Jonathan Edwards'). In 'Waking Early Sunday Morning' precision is expanded: as I hope to show later, while the stress words in 'Jonathan Edwards' have stress and thus significance simply because of selection, the stress words in this poem are significant because true, and ultimately reflecting an analogy between man and nature. *For the Union Dead*, which veered dangerously close to, but which, through concentration and power of thought and feeling avoided, the hedonistic doctrine of the equivalent significance of all phenomena, was influenced by William Carlos Williams as well as Gerard Manley Hopkins. In the 1961–62 *Hudson Review* Lowell explained his difficulty with Williams in a revealing way, 'It's as if no good poet except Williams had really seen America or heard its language'. One of the problems with Williams (as with Whitman) was the claim he made to a unique vision made objective by a generalised sense of the equivalent significance of phenomena, but he sometimes avoided the trap of that doctrine.

Lowell similarly avoided the trap in *For the Union Dead*, for reasons already explained. But the danger remained. Essentially, I suppose it is bound to be close to public poets like these two (America generalised was Williams's subject) because a framework of truth must be created out of phenomena to replace a lost framework, while, since the public urge is also a communal urge, all phenomena are material to the object of the work, and it is tempting to emphasise all. In the tight, short lines of *For the Union Dead* Lowell, within a limited range, could afford a stress that was local but generalised as well, but the line could not be extended—and hence inclusiveness of experience was impossible —without the collapse of the structure. Again, this is similar to the process of juxtaposition discussed earlier, and particularly to the practice of Hemingway (p. 61). Lowell had to appear to have selected, but could not be seen to select because everything, one way or another, was stressed. The sense of tragedy proceeding from his intellectual conception, which suffuses the poems, was the ultimate agent of synthesis; it showed that Lowell was a poet greater than his primitive medium; something of the same problem can be seen very clearly in the poems of Yvor Winters —very clearly because Winters was so crystal clear about his aims but lacked the poetic talent to impart the flowing sense of tragedy into his work.

It is curious to observe, in this discussion of influence, that both Lowell and Eliot were similarly influenced by Baudelaire. Accidie, as Winters said, was Baudelaire's subject, as it was Eliot's. Baudelaire devised a form within which he could judge his experience of it. Eliot, however, demonstrated rather than judged the feeling. Lowell has translated Baudelaire (published both in *Imitations* and in *The Voyage*) and, in a remark quoted from *The Spectator*, on the jacket of the 1968 English edition of *Life Studies*, Robert Hughes conveyed the quality of that translation in a description that has obvious relevance to *For the Union Dead*:

'Lowell would seem to have imitated the processes of Baudelaire's language with astonishing success. Words congeal, like ice, around an image and hold it in a kind of horrified isolation. . . .'

Something of this is shown in lines from *The Voyage* (dedicated, incidentally, to Eliot):

How sour the knowledge travellers bring away!
The world's monotonous and small; we see
ourselves today, tomorrow, yesterday,
An oasis of horror in sands of ennui!
Shall we move or rest? Rest, if you can rest;
move if you must. One runs, but others drop
and trick their vigilant antagonist.
Time is a runner who can never stop.

There can be no doubt of the importance to Lowell of the
practical study of form he made through translations and imitations. But it was all to serve a purpose of his own. Many
influences make themselves felt on him but, in the process of
experiment, refinement and development reaching its latest
climax in *Near the Ocean* it is, metrically, Hopkins who comes
back as the most powerful while, study and imitation apart,
the framework of action and tone Yeatsian, as the last stanza of the
title poem suggests:

Sleep, sleep. The ocean, grinding stones,
can only speak the present tense;
nothing will age, nothing will last,
or take corruption from the past.
A hand, your hand then! I'm afraid
to touch the crisp on your head—
Monster loved for what you are,
till time, that buries us, lays bare.

Briefly, the argument of 'Waking Early Sunday Morning'
proceeds as follows. In the first stanza (already quoted) the poet
observes the salmon and identifies with a struggle arduous and
ultimately fruitful. In the second the identification is extended to
nature but the joy felt by the poet is criticised as inadequate, however delightful, to the task of life. In the third stanza, nature,
admired, retreats before daylight and man. In the fourth the poet
surveys the busy world of daily life with regret for the loss of
dawn. In the fifth and sixth stanzas he expresses the wish that the
impulses of the morning could be blended with the quotidian

struggle for life into a tempered instrument and begins to inspect human frameworks of discipline where the impulse would find fruitful activity. The church is first among these frameworks. Its limitations—as corruptive of the pure strain of the natural impulse—are explored in the seventh stanza and in the eighth the poet resigns himself to seeking meaning in the wreck of human life and experience. Such meaning must, however, have a coherent source, a unity. In the ninth stanza this principle of existence is personified as God; but God seems unreachable through the evidences of human worship and history, which is the subject of the tenth stanza. In the eleventh the flow of energy from the original experience is choked off and a quieter rationality is tried and found wanting. In the twelfth stanza, therefore, the original impulse is re-evaluated and found crucial; it is given great public significance by association with the President of the United States. In the thirteenth stanza the inadequacy of both the President and available human discipline is summarised in a forceful but sad burst which precedes the climax of the last stanza, which I have already quoted.

This is a poem of remarkable beauty, comprehension and strength. One or two general points about it should be made. Its theme is not the beauty and goodness of nature or the natural impulse in man. Rather it is an account of an experience that brings home to the poet a consciousness of joy deemed to be good, followed by an attempt to find a way of injecting that good into the affairs of men. There is thus an analogy with nature, but the analogy is strictly defined and limited; it is a starting point; the real theme is the potentiality of man to achieve moral order. That the potentiality exists the poet has no doubt; whether contemporary man can make it fruitful is another question, to which a negative reply is given. But, in the remarkable last stanza, the awareness of potentiality is renewed and expressed in an infinitely tragic pre-diction: the prediction that awareness is all man can achieve and that joy is no longer his to gain. With this tragedy it may be possible to come to some kind of terms, but that is a hope expressed by the poet for the future: as the fourth and eleventh stanzas make clear, it is not for the poet himself.

The form of the poem, the longer line with a springing inner stress, which is sharpened in the selection of phenomena in the first stanza, and softened into a controlled but smoothly flowing sadness in the last, is integral to the account Lowell offers of experience. In the first stanza the reader will recall that sharp stress of sense in the lines. Note, however, the remarkable achievement of the second stanza: the first is distanced and placed by the rough irregular break of the first words of the stanza. Then Lowell proceeds with remarkable rhythm and control to render a living experience again through sense stress before the elevated blend of the last two lines. If the reader listens carefully he will hear the way in which the emphatic discipline of *For the Union Dead* has been extended into a controlled flow:

> Stop, back off. The salmon breaks
> water, and now my body wakes
> to feel the unpolluted joy
> and criminal leisure of a boy—
> no rainbow smashing a dry fly
> in the white run is free as I,
> here squatting like a dragon on
> time's hoard before the day's begun!

The last two lines are among the most beautiful effects Lowell has achieved. Yet already here, after the unconfined arduousness of the first stanza, we have a hint of the sadness that is to be the governing emotion remaining after the argument of the poem is completed.

The last two lines of the second stanza are Yeatsian. In the fourth stanza the rhythm is tightened to convey the bustle and disparate activity of the world of men. The kinship with Yeats is much more marked:

> Fierce, fireless mind, running downhill.
> Look up and see the harbour fill:
> business as usual in eclipse
> goes down to the sea in ships—
> wake of refuse, dacron rope,

> bound for Bermuda or Good Hope,
> all bright before the morning watch
> the wine-dark hull of yawl and ketch.

The extraordinary precision with which phenomena are described is, however, shown best in the first four lines of the next
stanza:

> I watched a glass of water wet
> with a fine fuzz of icy sweat,
> silvery colours touched with sky,
> serene in their neutrality—

This is the end of the first movement of the poem. By the
precision and discernment of his response and the communication
of so controlled and aware a sensitiveness to nature the poet has
established one point: that, in the uninterrupted and undefiled
presence of nature man feels a welling-up of joy which represents a force within him for happiness, that is, for good. The presence of this force, in the second to the fifth stanza, counterpoints
the observation of the first. The first stanza sees the final achievement of the salmon, within the cruel discipline of the salmon
ladder, the achievement so great that, after it, and after passing
the capacity to achieve it once again through spawning, death is
acceptable. It suggests an identification with that struggle but,
when the theme of 'O to break loose' is taken up again later on,
the poet becomes aware of the limitations of the analogy: nature
is a context for inspiration, it is not, ultimately, satisfactory in
itself. The predicament of man is that, unlike the salmon, his
discipline is not imposed: it has to be understood and therefore
made. The poet tries to reconcile his unconfined joy in nature
with this inescapable task:

> yet if I shift or change my mood,
> I see some object made of wood,
> background behind it of brown grain,
> to darken it but not to stain.

That is the aspiration—to employ the natural impulse justly in the service of contrived human order. In the next two lines that aspiration, so firmly defined here, becomes a cry which hints at the impossibility of Lowell achieving this ambition and communicates the agony the context of nature imparts when once the consciousness of this impossibility dawns:

> O that the spirit could remain
> tinged but untarnished by its strain!
> Better dressed and stacking birch,
> or lost with the Faithful at Church—
> anywhere, but somewhere else!

After this twisting and turning agony the church is confronted in a stanza that opens the way to the fine middle movement of the poem, which restates a theme familiar to Lowell—loss of faith by man conveyed by inability to understand the signs of religion and the consequent necessity of searching for new meaning in the detritus of life. One of the great strengths of the stanza dealing with the rejection of the church is the way in which the focus, emphasis and origins of rejection are made to lie within man— the Bible is 'chopped and crucified', and yet some nagging sense of the significance and meaning of the historical experience of religion remains:

> O Bible chopped and crucified
> in hymns we hear but do not read,
> none of the milder subtleties
> of grace or art will sweeten these
> stiff quatrains shovelled out four-square—
> they sing of peace, and preach despair;
> yet they gave darkness some control,
> and left a loophole for the soul.

Like Yeats

> I must lie down where all the ladders start
> In the foul rag and bone shop of the heart.

Lowell turns elsewhere:

> No, put old clothes on, and explore
> the corners of the woodshed for
> its dregs and dreck: tools with no handle,
> ten candle-ends not worth a candle,
>
> . . .
>
> the wordless sign, the tinkling cymbal.

But Lowell does not allow us to forget the single and coherent purpose of this search. It is to know God, and the tragedy of life lies in the gradual disappearance of the symbols of God. The next stanza fines itself down, both formally and in its argument, from the broadest comprehension of the purpose of man to the draining from the landscape of the evidence of that purpose. Again, the tone is simple, tragic, precise and majestic:

> When will we see Him face to face?
> Each day, He shines through darker glass.
> In this small town where everything
> is known, I see His vanishing
> emblems, His white spire and flag-
> pole sticking out above the fog,
> like old white china door-knobs, sad,
> slight, useless things to calm the mad.

Or, in one of Lowell's early and most unforgettable phrases:

> The breath of God had carried out a planned
> And sensible withdrawal from this land;

In the next stanza the violence, chaos and ultimate purposelessness of non-theistic human life is stated. The following stanza questions, suddenly, the poet's judgement but, with the refrain 'anywhere, but somewhere else' he is brought back to the perception that gave rise to his judgement. This in turn brings him back to the theme of yearning which suffuses the poem—'O to break loose'. The restatement takes place in a changed and elevated key

7*

for this is the stanza which introduces the President of the United States as a man, sharing the predicament and perception of the poet and raising the argument of the poem finally from the unique to the public. Like the poet, the President (specifically, Lyndon B. Johnson) is capable of awareness of the dilemma. He, too, can 'break loose' to the extent of reaching a point of insight into the predicament; he, too, cannot (as the second last stanza makes clear) 'break loose' from freedom to order and so cannot control the phenomena of evil unleashed in the world by human action. The stanza, indeed, defines the trap of the President's daily life at the same time as it conveys his moment of freedom:

> O to break loose. All life's grandeur
> is something with a girl in summer . . .
> elated as the President
> girdled by his establishment
> this Sunday morning, free to chaff
> his own thoughts with his bear-cuffed staff,
> swimming nude, unbuttoned, sick
> of his ghost-written rhetoric!

We then have a stanza of pure horror at the plight of the world before the last stanza which I have already quoted.

In this outline I have only touched on the local merits of this poem: I have not, for instance, mentioned the play upon words and concepts such as 'dark' and 'eclipse', nor the interplay of imagery—as in the last stanza quoted—which reflects the relationship between freedom and order. The real point about the poem is the dignity and precision of its language and the overall appropriateness of its rhetoric to the size and scope of its grand theme, together with the stoic sense of tragedy that informs the whole. The tragedy consists in the statement of man's capacity to see into, to seek out and define his predicament, to sense an absolute canon of judgement, an ultimate moral order, but to be able to channel his emotion, conviction and life force into the service of this intellectual comprehension. But the sensibility, finally, is one of tragedy, not despair. Lowell's conceptual and formal control is at its strongest and most subtle in the final stanza. One of the finest things about this stanza is, following the violence of its predecessor, its gentleness, compassion and understanding. Its résumé of the poem's themes is comprehensive, the hopes it has to offer limited; within the context of man's fate, however, its judgement is not only stoical but wise with the wisdom that comprehends and includes tragedy. Of all the fine poems Lowell has written this seems to me to be the finest, for it has no internal flaws; there can be no overall doubts about its nature, as with 'The Holy Innocents' and 'Mr. Edwards and the Spider'; and the form is expansive rather than limited, as in the case of *For the Union Dead*. If is is not as great a poem as, say, 'Sunday Morning' or 'The Course of a Particular', that lies in no fault of the poem, but, rather, in the superior control, complexity and range of Stevens's mind. This, moreover, is still a stage in Lowell's development, and it seems to me he has still further to go in his investigations of the human spirit.

The form of 'Waking Early Sunday Morning' is retained for the other poems in *Near the Ocean* which are major in intent and not imitations—'Fourth of July in Maine', 'The Opposite House', 'Central Park', and 'Near the Ocean' itself. All these are flawed in some way, however, as the new utterance falters uncertainly over the interpretation of some phenomenon. One of the finest effects comes in 'Near the Ocean':

> We hear the ocean. Older seas
> and deserts give asylum, peace
> to each abortion and mistake.
> Lost in the Near Eastern dreck,
> the tyrant and tyrannicide
> lie like the bridegroom and the bride;
> the battering ram, abandoned, prone,
> beside the apeman's phallic stone.

The first three lines of this stanza have something of Stevens about them: with a different meaning there is something of 'the old chaos of the sun' in these lines. But the inclusiveness promptly becomes generalised and the examples arbitrary and conflicting in meaning: the sensibility is intermittent.

Similarly in 'Fourth of July in Maine', a lament for Lowell's cousin Harriet Winslow, there is a stanza charged with the most precise and disciplined fatigue of soul, the purity and accuracy of its awareness encased in the strong, firm rhythmic beat of the lines which carry forward the sentiment and make it both universal and eternal. (The opposite conclusion, drawn from the same theme, can be seen in Yeats's 'Some burn damp faggots, others may consume/The entire combustible world in one small room'.)

> And here in your converted barn,
> we burn our hands a moment, borne
> by energies that never tire
> of piling fuel on the fire;
> monologue that will not hear,
> logic turning its deaf ear,
> wild spirits and old sores in league
> with inexhaustible fatigue

But much of the poem is imperceptive in the misplacing of stress

> in the cold oven, icy plates—
> repeating and repeating, one
> Joan Baez on the gramophone.

As with every stage of his successes, therefore, the balance of Lowell is precarious: at every stage of his career there is a lurking trap waiting to destroy him. In the case of Stevens the hedonism that ruins the great bulk of his poetry could be found lurking even in the great early poem, 'Sunday Morning', in the sixth stanza of which (as Winters saw) the projection of a hedonistic paradise involves the poet in proposing the indefinite and single-minded cultivation of the emotions which ultimately destroys the capacity of the artist to discriminate morally. Similarly the generalised and deliberate search for significance and meaning in phenomena invariably carried with it a danger that a moment will come when the poet will be unable to distinguish value: his own moral control will be dissipated.

I have suggested the contribution Lowell's forms make to the stabilisation of his moral control. But form is not all and its cultivation can betray him. These lines come from 'Central Park'

> each precious, public, pubic tangle
> an equilateral triangle,
> lost in the park, half covered by
> the shade of some low stone or tree.
> The stain of fear and poverty
> spread through each trapped anatomy,

'The stain of fear and poverty' is quite an unjustified line. It is neither prepared for nor followed up. It is one of several such arbitrary effects in a poem with an equally arbitrary and impressionistic conclusion

> We beg delinquents for our life.
> Behind each bush, perhaps a knife;
> Each landscaped crag, each flowering shrub,
> hides a policeman with a club.

The public concern and the intended significance of the poem is obvious, but they are not argued but presented. There is nothing of the strong, critical rationality, combined with a concentrated charge of the description of the physical essence of phenomena, that we get in 'Waking Early Sunday Morning'. Ultimately rational concentration is lacking in 'Central Park' while formal concentration, though loosened, is still there.

At each stage of his career, then, Lowell's distinct successes are accompanied by failure and flaw and by the presence of some kind of serious ideological threat to the basic moral architecture of his work, a threat, moreover, that he often seems to cultivate, either wilfully or because danger must be courted to rescue some advantage from its context: thus the presence of William Carlos Williams in *For the Union Dead*. Though I have offered various descriptions of the nature of these threats—descriptions appropriate to the relevant stage of Lowell's career—it seems to me nonetheless to be the case that, at its root, the threat is always the same. It is a threat founded on the dangers attending the undisciplined entry of the personality of the poet into the poetry. At its ultimate worst it leads to the worst excesses of irrationalism, Romanticism, hedonism and the cultivation of trivia: its general nature is discussed in Chapter One and particular local forms of it in subsequent chapters. The actual character of the danger involved, moreover, is increased by the collapse of the controlling tradition of moral reference established by the earlier tradition of English literature, which collapse initially instigated the entry of the poet into the poetry.

Perhaps the most remarkable thing about Lowell is not his individual successes at various stages of his career but the actual advance in general of his work shown particularly in *For the Union Dead* and *Near the Ocean* ('Waking Early Sunday Morning'). In the stages leading to this latest advance the most distinct characteristic of his work has been the *Imitations*. Imitations are, for Lowell, transformations of different poems from different languages and cultures, rather than translations. 'This book', Lowell says in his introduction to *Imitations*, 'was written from time to time when I was unable to do anything of my own.' He adds of his originals: 'Nothing like them exists in English, for the excellence of a poet depends on the unique opportunities of his own language.' Though they have flashes of interest most of the imitations do not have a substantial life of their own. Moreover, the approach to different languages and cultures was made (according to Lowell's introduction) in so many different ways, from widely different standpoints of knowledge and cultivation, that it seems to me to be profitless at this stage to pursue the method of adaptation in each instance in order to discover what Lowell might have learned from his models.

On the other hand, there is little doubt that the relationship between Lowell and the tradition of poetry in its widest sense is intimate and one feels, even without being able to compare imitation to original in detail, that the benefit to Lowell was, ultimately, substantial. The imitations are the one great technical thread running throughout Lowell's career, and they represent a deliberate apprenticeship on his part, a cultivated vocation for poetry, enjoying a separate existence—an educational existence—from his own work.

It seems to me that this concern is ultimately self-critical and represents the sense in which Lowell's devotion to the craft of poetry is pure, disinterested, concentrated and objective, the sense in which it is separate from and standing above the egocentric non-poetic and anti-poetic tendencies that intrude so frequently into his own original work. The pursuit of the imitations reminds us of the extent to which Lowell's triumphs are triumphs of will. There is a sense, of course, in which poetry and literature generally can be thought of as enjoying a separate existence—an existence on a different moral plane—from the human experiences, with or without order, on which it draws for substance and sustenance. The cultivation of such a belief is, however, dangerous, because it may tend to separate the poet from human nature, separate him from the human concerns of his species. This is a danger Lowell has often met and often fallen victim to; nonetheless, in the end, the failures that resulted from his falls may have well been worth the achievements purchased by his deliberate dedication.

That dedication has been given its most substantial, considered and sustained form in the *Near the Ocean* 'version' of Juvenal's Tenth Satire, on 'The Vanity of Human Wishes', a satire, moreover previously imitated both by Johnson and Dryden. This is one of the most faithful (to the original) of Lowell's imitations. Several points of interest arise in the comparison between Juvenal, Dryden, Johnson and Lowell.

The first arises in relation to Johnson's famous (or notorious) first couplet: here are the four versions (I shall give quotations of varying completeness and unmatching length, because of the variety of the presentations):

> Omnibus in terris, quae sunt a Gadibus usque
> Aurorum et Gangem, pauci dinoscere possunt
> Vena bona atque illis multum diversa, remota
> Erronis nebula. Quid enim ratione timemus
> aut cupimus
>
> —*Juvenal*

>Look round the Habitable World, how few
>Know their own Good; or knowing it, pursue.
>How void of reason are our Hopes and Fears!
>What in the conduct of our Life appears
>So well-design'd, so luckily begun,
>But, when we have our wish, we wish undone?
>   —*Dryden*

>Let observation with extensive view,
>Survey mankind, from China to Peru;
>Remark each anxious toil, each eager strife,
>And watch the busy scenes of crowded life;
>Then say how hope and fear, desire and hate,
>O'erspread with snares the clouded maze of fate.
>   —*Johnson*

>In every land as far as man can go,
>from Spain to the Aurora or the poles
>few know, and even fewer choose what's true.
>What do we fear with reason, or desire?
>Is a step made without regret?

The quality of Juvenal I am not competent to comment on, though I believe I can feel an imitation of his greatness. Dryden's lines attain a certain regretful dignity towards the end. Lowell's are flat and imitative in the bad sense. Johnson's however, have both an immense dignity and a distinctive intellectual cast from the outset. Coleridge savagely attacked the first couplet, rendering it as 'let observation with extensive observation survey mankind extensively',[2] and many critics preceded and followed him in that unfavourable judgement. Saintsbury seems to me, however, to have the essence of the matter in him when he rebukes Coleridge[3]

>'Observation may be either broad and sweeping, or minute and concentrated; Johnson specifies the former kind in the last half of the first line. Observation may be directed to men, to things etc.; it is to mankind he wishes it directed, and he says so in the first half of the second. Further, as this is too abstract, he gives the poetic and imaginative touch by filling in the waste atlas. . . .'

In other words Johnson dominates the intellectual character of
the adaptation from the outset. And the truth of Saintsbury's
observation can be seen in the precise but varying development
and direction of the subsequent lines. In Lowell's version (and in
Dryden's) there is no such dominance. Where Lowell has distinct
merit is in the sudden vividness with which he communicates a
perception he shares with the original as, in these lines, of the
arbitrariness of power

> 'But tell us,
> What was his crime, friend? Who were the informers?
> What witness swore away his life?' 'No witness!
> A wordy long epistle came from Capri.'
> 'Tiberius spoke, enough. I'll hear no more.'

'A wordy long epistle' is effective here in contrast to the arbitrary
brutality of the killing of Sejanus. But, like the other characters
in Lowell's version Sejanus is nowhere realised: nothing comes
alive in the poem except the general notion in the title. Compare
the above lines to Johnson's on Wolsey:

> In full-blown dignity, see Wolsey stand,
> Law in his voice and fortune in his hand:
> To him the church, the realm, their pow'rs consign,
> Thro' him the rays of regal bounty shine,
> Turned by his nod the stream of honour flows,
> His smile alone security bestows:
> Still to new heights his restless wishes tow'r,
> Claim leads to claim, and power advances pow'r;
> Till conquest unresisted ceas'd to please,
> And rights submitted left him none to seize.
> At length his sov'reign frowns—the train of state
> Mark the keen glance, and watch the sign to hate.

In truth, there is no comparison, given the subtlety and range
of Johnson's account. What Johnson gained from Juvenal was the
assent of the universalising judgement of a mighty tradition. I
would not underrate its importance for him, given his historical

context and awareness of the classics. But the distinctive features of Johnson's achievement in the lines above are to be seen principally in two points: the steady, marching emphasis on 'him' and 'his' in the lines and the controlling circle of the poet's range of moral judgement, extended to others than Wolsey, in the last couplet, a control that is introduced by the compelling, contemptuous irony of 'the train of state'—the same contrast being made between office and merit for Wolsey's enemies as for Wolsey. This is public poetry at its greatest.

Yet it depends, ultimately, not only on the moral control of Johnson, on an innate capacity to judge, but on the intellectual power manifested, the intellectual control established, in the opening lines. Sound moral judgement, Johnson says, is ultimately a matter of reason and of reasoning sensibility. Yet again the intense and even neurotic personality of Johnson enters into this as into all his great poems—but particularly into 'London'—and it is that which concerns us here, the entry of the personality into the business of public judgement.

I have already observed Lowell's difficulties in this respect and, in my animadversions on Yvor Winters earlier in this chapter, I have suggested that we have not fully understood either the nature of the problem we are dealing with or the nature of partially successful efforts to resolve that problem in For the Union Dead and Near the Ocean. Johnson seems to me, however, to be crucial to the discussion, not simply because he was the first major poet to suffer the problem but because of the decidedly rational and intellectual character of his solution; a rationality was used, that is, even if it was not fully understood. It complemented a great moral nature and a great sensibility: it complemented genius and was one of the facets of genius. That intellectual mastery, as opposed to a critically emotional development, that self-devised and sustained confidence, that constructed inner certainty, Lowell has not yet achieved. To a degree it is something that can be sought out: it may be the next stage of his development.

For there is now a difference between the precariousness of Lowell's present balance of achievement and the precariousness of his earlier balances. The faults to which he was subject then were

faults of conviction and faults proceeding from a failure to distinguish, at root, between the relative objectivity of the things he
believed in. His faults now are those of the implications of his kind
of achievement; that, unlike in the earlier phase of his career, he
is aware of his faults, I have suggested in the earlier part of this
chapter, in discussing the influence of William Carlos Williams.
The intelligence that is now defensive, that protects him from
the traps towards which his positive inspiration drives him, may
yet become positive and masterful. If it does I am convinced we
shall have an achievement like to that of Johnson.

I confess, finally, that I cannot answer the question posed at
the end of my first chapter. I do not believe that enough of us
have given enough of the right kind of critical attention to the
poetry of our own time for an answer that would not be egocentric to emerge. If, on the other hand, we do give enough of the
right kind of critical attention to the poetry of our own time—
that is, if we judge it against and in the light of the tradition, and
examine its emerging positive characteristics in the same light—
then it is just possible that we may set ourselves fair towards a
solution of the first stage of the problem, that is, we may begin
to know what the resources of public poetry are; and I do
not believe that anything I have said in this book, however harsh
my criticism of individuals may have been, can be considered as
other than lending support to the proposition that it is public
poetry we seek.

However, these final reservations and criticisms may seem
insignificant compared to the achievement of 'Waking Early
Sunday Morning'. In this poem I believe we see, not only a superb
and sustained achievement in public poetry, an achievement
marked by the greatest possible dignity and gravity and the most
profound sense of tragedy; I believe we also see, at the end of a
long struggle, a great triumph, and, further, that, in reading it,
we can mark not only the triumphant re-emergence of the line of
gravity, but the defeat of the imprecision and corruption which
has, in our time, so threatened, not only poetry, but discussion
of poetry as well. With 'Waking Early Sunday Morning' we
not only return to the presence of great poetry, but we mark, in

that presence, its deep involvement in the life of our times, the conduct of our affairs and the quality of our life and ideas as well. That triumph achieved, I profoundly hope, will be more important than the reservations at the end of my argument.

Notes

CHAPTER 1 An Unblemished Adam

1. R. P. Blackmur, *Language as gesture* (New York, 1952), p. 58.
2. M. L. Rosenthal, *The New Poets*.
3. *Encounter*, April 1968.
4. *The Review*, March 1969.
5. Reprinted in James Scully (ed), *Modern Poets on Modern Poetry* (London, 1966), p. 241.
6. '*Anna Karenina*' *and other essays*, p. 197f.
7. In the lecture 'Great Poetry' published in *Independent Essays* (London, 1963).
8. *In Defence of Reason* (Denver, 1947), p. 451.
9. *Ibid*, p. 151f.

CHAPTER 2 Poems 1938–49

1. See Cleanth Brooks, 'Poetry since "The Waste Land"', in *The Southern Review* (Summer 1965).
2. *The Modern Poet* (London, 1968), pp. 34–5.

CHAPTER 3 'The Quaker Graveyard' and 'The Mills of the Kavanaughs'

1. In *The English Mystical Tradition* (ed. London, 1964), pp. 2–3.
2. *Furioso* vi (Autumn 1951), p. 77.

CHAPTER 4 Life Studies

1. In Ian Hamilton (ed), *The Modern Poet* (London, 1968). *Beyond all this fiddle* is also the title of a collection of short pieces by Mr Alvarez.
2. In his remarks on Winters and Leavis in *Beyond all this fiddle*.

Notes

CHAPTER 6   Near the Ocean and Imitations

1. Helen Gardner, *The Art of T. S. Eliot* (London, 1949), p. 55.
2. Quoted in David Nichol Smith and E. L. McAdam (eds), *The Poems of Samuel Johnson* (Oxford ed. 1962), p. 30.
3. George Saintsbury, *A history of Criticism* (London ed. 1923) iii, 223, n. 1.

Bibliography

I have included here some important prose pieces by Lowell and some other writings on him, but not the general and well-known critical works mentioned in my text.

Blackmur, R. P.: *Language as Gesture* (New York, 1952).

Brooks, Cleanth: 'Poetry since "The Waste Land"', in *The Southern Review* (Summer 1965).

Fitts, Dudley: review of *The Mills of the Kavanaughs*, in *Furioso* VI (Fall, 1951).

Hamilton, Ian (ed): *The Modern Poet* (London, 1968).

Holloway, John: review of *Near the Ocean*, in *Encounter* (April 1968).

Lowell, Robert: review of *Four Quartets*, in *Sewanee Review* LI (Summer 1943).

'A Note on Hopkins', *The Kenyon Review* VI (Autumn 1944).

Review of William Carlos Williams, *Paterson: Book Two*, in *Nation* CLXVI (19 June 1948).

'Yvor Winters, a Tribute', in *Poetry* XCVIII (April 1961).

Interview in James Scully (ed): *Modern Poets on Modern Poetry* (London, 1966).

Mazzaro, Jerome: *The Poetic Themes of Robert Lowell* (Ann Arbor, 1965).

Pearson, Gabriel: 'Robert Lowell', in *The Review* (March 1969).

Staples, Hugh B.: *Robert Lowell: the First Twenty Years* (London, 1962).

Index

Index of Persons and Poems

The published volumes of Robert Lowell are listed on page 13. Also indexed are individual poems when discussed at any length in the text.